Notes from JOHN:

Messages from Across the Universe

By Marcia McMahon, M.A.

John, Across the Universe, watercolor © by Marcia McMahon, M.A. all rights reserved.

Eternal Rose Publishing

ISBN 978-0-9766477-2-0

Previous books by Marcia McMahon, M.A.
Princess Diana's Message of Peace,
An Extraordinary Message of Peace for Our World.
Sweet Grass Publishing, ISBN:0-9723376-2-8
Write to Print,© 2003.
With Love from Diana, Queen of Hearts:
Messages of from Heaven for a New Age of Peace,
© 2005. ISBN: 0-9766477-0-2
Eternal Rose Publishing ©. All rights reserved
www.dianaspeakstotheworld.com

Dedication

I dedicate this book, first and foremost to the Beatles and the great energies they brought to the planet with music, love and world peace. I further dedicate this book to the memory of the great John Winston Ono Lennon.

Notes of Thanks

I would personally like to thank Robert Murray of thestarsstillshine.com and for his collaborative effort in putting together this book, for his messages contained herein from John, and his truly amazing musical creations that were part of this ongoing project!

I would also like to thank many members of the JL group online by 1st name only. I thank Shelly, Jane. Patricia, Julian and really everyone who has been supportive to me while writing and editing this book. I would also like to personally thank Mary Mageau and Dorothy Mercer for their help in editing this book. I thank Dr. Todd Austin for his encouraging words about my messages from John. Last but not least I thank Don Newsome, producer of the radio network, BBS radio, for giving me the break to create a weekly show called the Peaceful Planet show, on www.bbsradio.com for some five years.

Testimonials

As a fellow channeler, I can attest to the complete honesty of Marcia's communication with the late John Lennon. Although I don't often use the vernacular expressions in my personal writings, I feel that I must use the expression "She nailed it" for the tone, expressions and atmosphere of John's voice as it comes through her. Not doing any name dropping (oops, I'm about to) I've "talked" to John Lennon and have been inspired enough to write some music in the John Lennon style. I can't say that John Lennon actually wrote the music and sent it to me because of copyright laws.

So he influenced me and he influenced Marcia to write lyrics to those songs. The music is mentioned in this book and it is one more aspect, side if you will, of John Lennon. He was and in my opinion, still is, one of the most talented musicians of the last century.

Marcia captures the essence of John Lennon and has placed him within the pages of this book. This is one case where a two dimensional book gives a multi-dimensional mind picture of a truly historic character with the Earth name of John Lennon.

Way-to-go Marcia!

Bob Murray

February, 2010

Murray, R. personal communication, 2010.

www.thestarsstillshine.com

***

We feel the Messages from John are very relevant to the war-torn state of the world today, especially where he says: 'Please turn on to peace before it's too late.' This is a message many people need to hear. And we love the positive message of the Peaceful Planet lyric:

Live in love and peace today, and

You'll have done your part

In creating the peaceful planet.'

Joanna Prentis and Stuart Wilson, co-authors of "The Magdalene Version" published by Ozark Mountain Press *www.ozarkmt.com*

***

I met Marcia via email in 2007 when I was actively seeking out other channels in contact with John Lennon's spirit. I found it incredible that we both had experienced not just communications from John, but also a shared a connection with the spirit of Princess Diana. At the time, this truly amazed me, because up to then, it seemed that afterlife conversations with the Princess were not reported much by people in the spiritual field. So to meet someone in contact with the *same two spirits* was really something to me.

Marcia has worked tirelessly over the years to bring her channeled messages to the public, both on radio shows and in print. Despite having other full time jobs and then suffering debilitating illnesses, she has persevered, and for that she should be awarded a medal!

The spiritual messages Marcia receives are quite different from my own experience (as well as the type of requests for work to be published) however; the *style of confirmation* she receives from her Guides is similar to my own. For example, humming the lyrics to a John Lennon song, then seeing those words on an envelope minutes later, raise goose bumps, and has to be more than simple coincidence. No doubt we are all "one" and in this together; John Lennon works with many Earthly subjects, for different purposes. Manifesting the vision he sets forth to us is one way of achieving "peace." We may never see *world* peace, but *inner* peace attained through union with our Higher Selves is a road to that end.

Shelley Germeaux

National John Lennon Examiner, www.john-lennon-news.com***

Dear Marcia,

Thanks for the work that you do with Beatle John to try to bring peace to this war crazed world. I love the book and especially feel both honored and privileged to have had the opportunity to hear some of John Winston Ono Lennon's finest works from the other side in both "Peaceful Planet" & "Radical Dolphin". Keep up the excellent work!

Love, light & life,

Dr. Todd W. Austin, http://atlantis92.blogspot.com/

http://www.facebook.com/Atlantis92

***

Jane McComber, author of Ruth Montgomery Writes Again!

I have had the pleasure of knowing Marcia McMahon for about two years now and have been privilege to her work channeling John Lennon. I have been channeling John Lennon myself for almost nine years. Marcia's work with John to bring peace and love to the world has been very similar to my own. He has conveyed to Marcia, as he has to me, that music is one of the best ways to reach the world. It is a language we all understand. He knew this when he was "alive," and he is still trying to bring his music through from the other side by channeling with Marcia and Bob Murray. I have channeled George Harrison as well, like Marcia, and I believe these two great souls are very genuine in wanting to help the world with their music, even if in an unconventional way. If some of you are thinking that John never did things in a conventional way, well then, this is even more proof to me that this message is real!!! John did things his way while on earth, and he is still doing things his way while on the other side! One gift that Marcia has that I don't have is the artwork that accompanies her writing. She is very talented artistically and I love that she not only captures John with her words, but her artwork as well.

Marcia is very honest and candid about how this came to be, which is a breath of fresh air. Her honesty about not being a musician herself is refreshing. And probably one of the reasons John and George chose her. She has integrity and she's not trying to hide anything. Marcia tells it like it is.

Her honesty about being nervous when meeting the Pete Best Band made me recall many moments when I felt the same way. Yet she took her work seriously and went on with it, despite her anxieties. Her goal is not trying to sell herself; it is trying to promote peace. She even has a radio show, which is called; "Peaceful Planet" I find that Marcia's channeling with John is very sincere. She captures his personality to a tee. The tone, expressions, and fond names such as " dear" and "babe" are right on. The way he says, "Luv ya" and "Caio" are things which I have experienced as well. John's essence is captured beautifully in Marcia's writing. She nails his sense of humor on the head. I find it incredible sometimes when I read her messages because they are so much like the ones I get from John. There is no doubt in my mind it is John Lennon This is genuine work, and genuine John Lennon. Of that I am certain.

Jane Macomber, author and John Lennon psychic, www.janemacomber.com

www.ruthmontgomerywritesagain.com

TABLE OF CONTENTS

PART ONE:

MESSAGES FROM THE LATE JOHN LENNON

World Peace, Music, Love and Ascension

Don't Forget to Listen to the Beatles. How the Messages Began and the True Story of our Connection to John Lennon

We all remember John Lennon's wonderful music and contribution to the peace movement in the 1960s. *Imagine* was a truly great song and his debut of world peace with Yoko on his honeymoon highlighted his intentions. Well, imagine that his intentions for world peace do go on! Imagine that John Lennon is speaking from the other side through a number of channels that share his vision of a world without war and fear. "Imagine all the people, living life in Peace;"… Now imagine that John actually contacted two different channels living in two different countries, for a single purpose—imagine that!

John Lennon began his contact with me some seven years ago while I was working on a painting. I had been a channel/medium for many years previously and heard from many other 'famous' and not so famous souls on the other side. This was my first message from John Lennon and his presence was unmistakable. He was apparently trying to give me some encouragement for my first book, not yet published entitled Princess Diana's Message of Peace.

Message from John Lennon on Music and Creativity

Channeled sometime in 2003

John: Be glad you're still in the flesh. We make great music here but there are no producers to get it out. You'll get the word out; the world is ready for your message. It wasn't ready for mine, but you know it's the same message: LOVE!

Marcia: Thank you, John. I am very honored.

J: We're trying to spare you your self-imposed suffering, the idea that your words of Princess Diana and Mother Teresa won't be listened to. That's all nonsense going round in your pretty little head.

You are a great channel, and we're happy for you. You don't know how lucky you are!

Me: Again, John, thank you.

J: You're welcome. And remember to listen to old Beatles songs. There's a great deal of wisdom there.

M: Oh, I do and I will. I've always loved you and the Beatles.

J: See, I told you it would happen!

Notes: That last line was added a few weeks later by John, after finding my first publisher for the first book I produced, entitled **Princess Diana's Message of Peace**: An Extraordinary Message of Peace for Our Current World (available from www.dianaspeakstotheworld.com).

As though planned by Heaven, my career as a psychic channel began to build slowly in my work with Princess Diana in her message of peace. I went on to publish both ***Princess Diana's Message of Peace,*** and two years later ***With Love from Diana, Queen of Hearts;*** *Messages from Heaven for a New Age of Peace* (McMahon, 2003, 2005).

According to Princess Diana, her messages through me, as written in my book, will totally prevent another terrorist attack on America. Princess Diana's work is focused on political solutions to peace. While she is a princess of peace, she works through words alone to save the world. It has been an amazing process to see the miracles she has worked through my own pen. But that is another story. My work as a channel is to bring peace to the planet. Here is an excerpt from my messages from Princess Diana on John's music channeled in October of 2001.

Princess Diana: "He was a prophet in his own time and his words echo in the hearts and minds of many on the earth plane and throughout eternity as well. He influenced the magnetic grid surrounding the world - so powerful was his words and music! He was a transformer in the human race and so was I, in my life as Diana, Princess of Wales. One heart and one heartbeat at a time and the '*world can be as one*' in the words of the great lyric poet, John Lennon, who is with me in spirit from time to time." (McMahon, M.A., 2001)

John's words and lyrics as channeled from the afterlife now, as he explained it, are supposed to feed into the collective mass consciousness, just as the mainstream consciousness knows every word to the Beatles' songs. The one caveat to that is that John's recent lyrics are being delivered telepathically via a channel, but with the same objective: to create peace through music and lyrics by making it a huge phenomenon, to drum it into the subconscious collective mind.

I would say John did a great job the first time with his musical talent. No doubt about it, we can all sing along to *Imagine* or *Give Peace a Chance*. No doubt about it, people know the lyrics and identify with them. He had great talent and with the Beatles, great potential for reaching mass consciousness. John did mention that the Beatles paved a way for ascension.

John's inspired lyrics are equally powerful now as channeled. Yet when he is not physically present that can present challenges to the mass consciousness for those stuck in the third dimension. To their thinking, John Lennon is 'dead' and couldn't possibly write another lyric. So my project with John Lennon is taking a whole lot longer than it would if he were still here in the physical; but then it would not be my project, but his. In this Bob Murray and George Harrison share it not only by myself, but also in a fusion of energies and consciousness. But the fact that he isn't here, but the lyrics are, to me gives ample testimony to the fact of Spiritualism and the truth of life after death.

I first experienced this process in prayer and meditation some twenty years ago; and anyone can learn to hear from their higher self. I believe anyone can tune in to their higher self, although some people are better at tuning, or listening, than others. While some people do hear the Voice of God or conscience they choose to ignore it or never mention it for the obvious reasons.

As one progresses through the stages of initiation into the higher dimensions, one must learn to listen with greater and greater attention to detail, nuance and skill; because, speaking only for myself, I hear no voice. It is really more that the words flow through my pen and mind and my typing to produce the messages and John's lyrics. Lyrics to songs and

6

diplomatic solutions for peace, as in the case of my work with Princess Diana, have all flowed through my mind and pen. Mine is a combination of automatic writing and channeling. Full channeling can involve the use of the voice of the channel while in a trance, where the entity speaks through the voice of the channel. That is not my style, but again, all are equally valid messages from the afterlife. While I do work with trance states in my hypnosis practice, I prefer my work to be done in full consciousness, while alert and awake. Hence I have a voice in the messages and act as an interviewer with John and others I speak with.

One friend asked me how it felt and I said it felt like I was connecting to another dimension. I would term it the fifth or sixth dimension; where we are all collectively heading, according to Dr John Jay Harper (Harper, J., 2007.) Dr Harper's excellent book, entitled *Trance formers, Shamans of the 21st Century* is a wonderful compilation of his esoteric and scientific knowledge about the phenomenal ascension we are about to experience. I suggest anyone with a casual interest in this topic read his work!

Channeling actually feels like a kind of stream of consciousness that I think everyone has tried at least once in his or her lifetime. Let your thoughts just flow—you will see what I mean if you still in quiet meditation and just begin writing. Set up a white light of protection to surround yourself before trying this or take lessons from a practiced channel if questions arise.

In May of 2005 John began to "send" me his messages and lyrics to songs in my writing. I was really amazed. It is a process in which I "receive telepathically" thoughts and impressions as I am sitting at the computer; much like automatic writing. Sometimes I am conscious. When I channeled a few words into a song called *Life goes on,* he asked me to contact Bob Murray immediately, saying Bob would be amazed. I followed up on John's suggestion.

Bob had been channeling a number of well-known celebrities on the other side for many years, including Diana, Elvis, Michael, his deceased son in law, and Ernest Hemmingway. (Murray, R. 2004)

In our regular monthly emails, I mentioned and shared the lyrics that John had given in a message that I faithfully recorded in May of 2005. Bob, or Fr. Murray as he is affectionately known, wrote back cryptically: "JOHN has something he wants to share with you, Marcia!" And he left it at that.

I was thinking it was another message; it turned out to be much more. In late May 2005, I was just getting out of school for the summer, where I was a professor of art history. I went to check my P.O. Box. Suddenly, without any reason at all, the words and music of the Beatles' song *With Love from Me to You* popped into my head, and I heard John say in his very Liverpool accent, "With Love from Me to You, Marcia my dear."

I went to the post office box and placed my key in it; unlocking a pile of junk mail, I thought nothing of it. But under the heap of junk was a small package from Bob Murray. I opened it, and it was a garage band CD by Bob Murray, called *With Love from John.* I was floored. Breathless, I jumped into the car and thrust the CD straight into the player. The first tune of the sixteen or so songs was titled *Peaceful Planet!* I couldn't believe my ears!

I was stunned with excitement! John was writing through Bob Murray and me! How cool, I thought. I knew we shared a Diana connection and he had sent many messages from Princess Diana to me personally via email, and they are published in my book, ***With Love from Diana, Queen of Hearts.*** I knew what I was hearing was the real deal, John's style and all. I knew I had heard John's lyrics; but here was something really extraordinary. Or was it? I held the CD in my hand. It coincidentally said, "With love from John" - exactly the lyrics I had in my mind a moment ago. Coincidence? I don't believe in them anymore.

So when John told me two and one-half years ago I was 'about to go really big,' I thought, 'Wow, sounds great!' I do not have an agent or a big book deal. I doubted John's words and myself. Who wouldn't doubt that? But my guides have told me that my work with Princess Diana will one day be known worldwide.

This project with John and George (Harrison) came about through his contact through me; and then separately through Bob Murray at exactly the same time, May of 2005. Coincidence—we both began receiving messages, in my case lyrics at the same time as Bob Murray caught on to hearing music of some form from them on the other side.

I asked John about coincidence and it was a confirmation that we were indeed on to something grander than we could ever imagine if you'll pardon the pun. He encouraged the correspondence and entire project. We're getting to all that.

John had contacted Bob Murray and me at the very same time separately, for the very same reason, as he put it, to 'Give Peace a chance.' Neither Bob Murray nor I could be making this up and the fact that it occurred at the same time gives credence to the contact from the spirit realms. The reader may doubt, but often one must also register the timing and coincidence of such things.

I certainly never set out to be a channel for the greatest musical lyricist in all of the twentieth century, John Lennon. I also need to clarify: I have no musical talent, so the lyrics are not complete without being sung and performed. I am sure Bob did not set out to channel John's music either. By the way, Bob is also a teacher by trade and has no formal musical training. The key for us as mediums is being open to the spirit. In my past work with Princess Diana, I found that usually when spirit requests something, there is something of great importance to humanity that needs to be accomplished. I am merely the pen to the spirit wanting to write through me. John assures me in these writings that he is attempting to create peace on the earth plane once more.

After all, we were in another war, in Iraq at the time, with so much of the same controversy that we had in Vietnam, a war John protested against. John told me later that he has many so-called "enlightened souls" with whom he works on the earth plane, to paraphrase his words. We are getting to his words; bear with me, dear reader, as more of the story unfolds. I believe John's thoughts and intentions are eternal and profound impulses to world peace, just as when he walked and sang here.

Some five months later, while being interviewed on BBS radio.com, the producer noticed a very high listener audience during my first live interview on the *Rochelle Sparrow's Psychic Connection* show, and the producer offered me a new radio show based on the performance during the first radio interview on BBS radio (originally at www.blogginservice.com). This came about at the very start of the BBS network, which has grown to be the number one New Age radio network! What a fortuitous event that was! Was this arranged by spirit, I began to wonder?

As fate would have it, I was given a radio show on which I could get the music out, as John put it in that first message to me about his music on the other side. So you see spirit had a plan all along for John, for Diana, for their work through me and for the creation of peace on earth. Even in that first message he indicated a deficiency in producers on that side; I guess they had all gone to a hotter place! All kidding aside, in heaven there is no money to be made so that is the real reason why no one takes on the rough jobs like being a producer. (No offense to any of you music producers out there, just a little humor.)

My radio show came along and this is what John had to say:

"We're going to Rock and Roll the Beatles Once Again, Marcia my dear, on your show. It's going to be the best show on the BBS network if I don't say so me, due to our music…"

Those were the words of a very excited John Lennon from spirit, when he found out I would host a show; he in fact he told me as much before I was offered the show. The following is the full message from John:

We're Going to Rock and Roll Once Again on Your Show!

Channeled by Marcia McMahon March 4, 05

John: Yeah, we've been waiting for a long time, really, more than just the six weeks or so. For me it's been many years and many tears, and we are finally rock and rollin' the Beatles again on your show! We can't stress enough how pleased we are with your show, Marcia; the Forum for World Peace, for it not only fits Diana's beautiful work, but ours. My music will again be heard on earth thanks to you and others working with me, namely Murray and now Chris Moors. He has a sound that is so much like me and he does channel me now and then. Just trust this won't go unnoticed, my dear. You're going to go to the top sooner than you think. And we're pleased to be working with other light workers who stand for peace everywhere! (McMahon, M. 05)

M: I wanted to ask you about whether I should include your messages in my Ascended Masters pages on the website or in your own name, John?

13

John: Oh that again. Well as far as being an Ascended Master, I don't wish to be worshipped or put on any religious pedestal. You all know my feeling about religion being a big problem on this planet. My idea is to bring oneness and unity through my music as always. I am aware of the ascension process for the whole planet, yeah. All of us who stood for peace and love on the planet were leading the way towards Ascension even in the 60s with the Beatles music we did.

Of course, I am of the Ascension movement. But please don't call me an Ascended Master cuz that would have connotations of people calling on me for protection or other things, and frankly I do work with a number of enlightened souls on the earth plane, but mainly my focus is for peace, Marcia my dear. So we'll leave it at that for now. Though since arriving here, of course, I am made aware of there being a God and a wonderful afterlife. We now work with the ascension energies and of course Diana is a master in her own right as are the others you work with. We're all working on this big planet together to bring about peace before its too late, ya know! Well, we'll be listening in the upstairs studio

this evening and we congratulate ya on your new time slot and

New Show. We're gonna rock and roll the Beatles and we

hope all the best for Bloggin Service and those wonderful light

workers, Don and others who are behind it!

Ciao for now,

LUV ya, John

Notes: Blogging Service was the original name for www.bbsradio.com and the one station I started with. I have been on air now for going on three years (BBSradio.com, 2005).

We now feature the musical work of Bob Murray as inspired by the spirit of John and George on my show each week, and I have been channeling their lyrics by listening to Bob's music. I now have a collection of over thirty songs with the most fantastic lyrics, some of which will be included in this book. We do not actually claim it to be John Lennon, however due to the fact that it is inspired by him, but we own the copyright. The genius of the lyrics is all John from spirit— I believe the same spirit of John Lennon, and that is why when you find them you will see a similarity. There is no intent to do a sound alike or "just like the Beatles" thing in this work, since again I am not musical and neither is Bob Murray. We are both talented psychic channels, though, and I believe that is why John chose this collaborative idea.

There are too many songs, and remember I have no musical ability! But I have included the lyrics in a separate section of this book for your enjoyment. Check out Bob's site and my site; then be open to the music from Robert Murray at www.thestarsstillshine.com

Each week the *Peaceful Planet Show* features music as synthesized from spirit through the medium-ship of both Bob and myself, lyricist for the spirit communication from John Lennon. This is the marquee for our *Peaceful Planet* show:

OUR MUSIC is synthesized from SPIRIT!

Through the medium-ship of Robert Murray

Inspired by John and George,

Frank De Vol, and Michael and the Band!

Visit www.thestarsstillshine.com. (McMahon, M. 2008)*

Now, it's not the Ed Sullivan Show, but I take great pride that I can introduce John and George, the *Half Beats*, as they are now known in heaven, to the world on my show. Many of their songs are about saving the Earth, ascension and other current topics. Each week new songs are created and performed via synthesized music in mp3 format for the edification of the small listening audience. Of course, if the planet only knew Each Divine Mind wants something done, it finds a way. Peace will come to earth thanks to the many souls on the other side working to bring it in whatever way possible.

We do feel inspired by John Lennon and other souls who continue their music on the other side. We frequently offer new music all for free, not charging in any way for it.

At some point John has said he wishes our copyrighted material to reach the mass consciousness like he did while living. While we do not wish to imitate any of The Beatles or his work with Yoko, we encourage our listeners to be the judge of the musical sounds, which are familiar in tone, lyrics and style to the late John Lennon and George Harrison. We are not tied to any of their former families and wish not to offend them in any way; nor are we interested in financial gain, having any association with the former ex Beatles who own their own copyrights. We are doing this solely for the purpose of the edification of our listeners and those open to the process of channeling. If this is not your thing, you don't have to read further.

References:

Harper, J., www.johnjayharper.com, Trance formers: Shamans of the 21st Century.

Reality Entertainment TV. www.realityentertainment.tv

McMahon, M. **With Love from Diana, Queen of Hearts, Messages from Heaven for a new age of Peace. Published 2005**. Page 61, John Lennon on Creativity and Diana's Message (With Love from Diana.) C. McMahon all rights reserved. www.dianaspeakstotheworld.com

Murray, R. www.thestarsstillshine.com Home of the Stars still shine, an Afterlife Journey by Robert Murray, and the ezine, The Stars Still shine Ezine by Robert Murray.

All rights reserved, ©. 2008 Fr. Bob Murray. His deceased son-in-law, Michael, who works with John and George, and knows Princess Diana, affectionately calls him Fr. Bob Murray instead of just Bob. Robert Murray is creating all this music from the other side with many talents, not just John and George. He has an ability to "hear" the music that spirits are creating and to write the tunes through a Band in the Box program in a computer. If you were to listen to his songs on the website, you will hear that they sound remarkably clear and true to form of the style of John, George, and even people like Louis Armstrong. Our project came together under what we feel was John's direction to help bring the music of heaven to the earth plane and assist people everywhere with peace. We have never charged for this project and want people to enjoy it and turn on to peace. If you have never checked out Bob's wonderful site please do so now so you can turn on to

peace and tune into the great music he is doing, at
www.thestarsstillshine.com

Find the music section, under the Magical Musical Tour.

Newsome, D. www.bbsradio.com if Internet Radio has a
name it's BBS radio, the Number 1 Internet Radio station
worldwide. Originally conceived by Don and Doug Newsome
and called www.Blogginservice.com

Retrieved Feb, 2008 my show was originally titled the
Forum for World peace. It is now known thanks to the gentle
nudging of a certain person in spirit, as the **Peaceful Planet**,
as you will read it was all John's idea! **The Peaceful Planet
Show** offered a variety of New Age topics from music to
ascension, as well as Princess Diana's words on world peace.
Our goal is to return the world to peace as envisioned by the
Divine plan. One radio show is not enough to do that.
However the intentions of peace in such a war torn world
cannot be mitigated to a trivial pursuit.

John's Music with George on the Other Side

M: John, how is the music going with George these days? And send my love to George too.

J: Oh, yea we're on some synthesized music now and still working with Murray.

John: Marsh, what about Bloggin Service? Maybe they'd post the lyrics and Murray could sell the music and you the lyrics for a small fee? If presented in a service format there we might be able to rock and roll the Beatles again ya know!

M: John, you're brilliant.

I'm going to write to Bob to find out what he thinks.

John: While you're at it give Bob this message:

Don't worry about a thing, Bob!

Bob when Yoko sees it, she'll get it!

I'm working through and she's working with Paul now. There's going to be a big break for ya real soon, so keep up the good work!

LUV Ya,

John

John's Peaceful Planet- How the Show Got Its Name!

Channeled May 20, 2005 by Marcia McMahon

M: Just saying hello to ya John.

J: Yeah we are hearing you loud and clear over here Marcia. Long time no channeling, babe. We miss ya and want to do more work on the lyrics whenever you're ready. We realize that you might be needing a little vacation before we commence our work but this will not be in vain, as I said before you are about to go really big and BBS will be a part of this endeavor. We in spirit want to put the word out about our music and lyrics through you and we want you to be clear about your objectives.

M: Well I am clear about that John. I have many issues going at the moment but intend at some point to ask Don for the show back, and maybe format it a little differently. I am thinking of calling it Forum for World Peace again but leave out the Princess Diana, not her or her message but just the name, and add in maybe the Ascended Masters.

21

J: What about calling your show "The Peaceful Planet," in honor of my song and your message? I think that would get the idea of your work with Diana, and me to the attentions of a major producer while conveying the same idea as always. It's always about the sale and production and in essence you compromise nothing. I would not forgo any of your work with Diana but I would bring in the other masters you work alongside besides me. While we have a ways to go on the lyrics, I do see that happening this summer for you luv. So keep the faith and just trust me when I say you're about to go really big.

Let Don know of my intentions to bring out my music once more and as Chris said, "Johnny will pull some strings" and not only that, play some strings for the show.

Get on with it then and let Don and his brother know about your future with BBS.

Diana may have her reservations of course about her work being welcome but we see no apparent conflict with this Forum for Peace. All we are saying is give PEACE a chance!

22

Thank you for listening to me. I am going back to the

studio; George and I are playin a new tune today.

Thanks much and God bless,

Luv ya,

Ciao

John

Notes: So this is how my show got its title and the music on the show came to be. By listening to spirit guidance, as John suggested these ideas, as my opportunities began to manifest on the earth plane, John's ideas began to influence my work and some of his predictions about getting the show and working with Don and Doug Newsome came to be realized. However the whole bit about going big has yet to have materialized; and that, I think, is largely the hesitancy I have had in moving forward. I personally never set out to "go big" using John's name, and although that is what these messages say- it was always my intention to remain the messenger, and not the celebrity behind the message. Bob Murray is extremely humble and with both of us rather shy we have been hesitant to publish our work with John because of the immense public scrutiny that will be out there. Nonetheless, these are the messages and they are what John said, his after death communication to me, about his intentions. So I am doing my part to honor John by being his scribe and I hope it does not offend his living family. When they read the messages perhaps they will see the obvious—that I could not be making this up; nor could Bob Murray—and that they are from John with love! What an exciting path to take- and one I never dreamed possible. But I only hope one day the music will be heard around the world again, to celebrate the coming of the golden age of peace of man. For if ever there was a worthier goal, I cannot think of that one of world peace.

All We are Saying is Give Peace a Chance!
Channeled 2005

M: Hi John--Saying hello to you!

John: Yeah Marcia, it is time for this debut of my new music and George's. Bet you weren't expecting this but we are glad and honored to be your featured guests!

M: Spirit has a way, John, of making things work for the best. I was to do another Mother Mary show and feature more on the Da Vinci code. But people grow bored with that theme too.

John: There's nothing boring in any of your shows Marcia. You're a great host and we are honored to be on today. We'll be watching from the upstairs studio. I believe Diana has a message she's wanting to bring thru you tonight so do be open. She's right here with me tugging my arm. It's all about the situation in the Middle East. For all those listeners we want to turn people on to your wonderful work with the great Princess Diana.

Her work is most important for without peace, the whole entire planet cannot fully enter into Ascension, as she understands it. We of the Ascension movement, and the Beatles were of the Ascension movement and began it all really, we stood up for peace. We stood up for non-violence, and we ask all for no more war. All we are sayin is give peace a chance. This very idea of antiseptic wars, where buttons are pushed remotely while children die is just as bad as the whole ludicrous notion of terror in the name of one's God. There is a God here and we want people the world over turned on to peace.

Imagine peace, Imagine love, imagine that your world is about to totally transform to this love vibration.

Well enough of my ranting. I'll let Diana have her say.

All we are saying is give peace a chance.

Luv ya,

John

Thanks to Fr. Bob Murray
From John. Channeled 2005

Marcia: Hey John, saying hello to ya finally and big, big thank you!

John: Oh, you needn't thank me for all your hard work with Diana and others, myself included. Hey, big Congratulations on your new show! It's going to be really a big hit and we feel it's gonna land you some kind of contract deal—book deal. Also we want to thank you for bringing up Fr. Bob Murray as the first guest on your show and highlighting my new music from the other side!

We're really excited about sharing our latest hits from the other side with Planet Earth to bring more peace awareness, and of course to continue our creative efforts.

We want to see the people of earth turned on to peace is all I'm saying.

M: I apologize I have not been able to channel the lyrics in months; I had set December as a time for you John. Oddly enough, so had Spirit apparently!

J: Just know we love you and Diana lots and do let Bob know you intend to bring up your messages with his appearance so that the audience can get that this stuff we're producing. Producers or not it is real love, peace and joy this Christmas Season to all.

Luv ya,

John

PS Don't forget some good Beatles music on the interview will draw in interest right away.

References:

Murray, R. retrieved 2005, www.thestarsstillshine.com

Bob Murray's deceased son-in-law Michael, who works with John and George on the other side, knows Princess Diana, and affectionately calls him Fr. Bob Murray instead of just Bob. Robert Murray is creating all this music from the other side with many talents, not just John and George. If you have never checked out Bob's wonderful site please do so now so you can turn onto peace and tune into the great music he is doing, at www.thestarsstillshine.com

Find the music section, under the Magical Musical Tour Music home page:

http://www.TheStarsStillShine.com/music.html

Imagine Peace, Imagine Love!
Channeled December 17, 2006 by Marcia McMahon

Marcia: Hi John, I'm hearing yaw, and want to say a big thank you for sending on more of your great tunes, like Outstretched Arms and George's songs for our program.

John: Yeah we're going to rock and roll the Beatles once more dear on your show. Pardon me saying so but it's going to be the very best show on the Blogging site!

M: John when I look and see your words from just a few weeks ago how right on your words were with Blogin-service. You, John correctly predicted that and also knew it would result in something big. And just like you said, boom it's big!

J: Yeah we all knew you'd be making it sometime soon and your message from Diana is truly great just as she was. We want ya heard you know.

M: We were in the midst of speaking of how to approach Yoko and ask her permission to do this project and to convince her of my genuine connection to you, something that will give her no doubt that this is really you. And then you gave me the mental picture of the Double Fantasy Album the one you and she did before your leaving us all in the terrible way you did.

John: As I was saying, I used to keep house and Yoko did a lot of the business. I used to tidy up the house and keep the kids. It was a crazy life really cuz I spent a lot of my time doing family things and working up late at night, like you're doing now.

M: Well I love the new music John, and I can't tell you the honor is all mine to debut yours and George's great stuff. And by the way, tell George his new songs really rock and roll and they're superb! Not that my compliment means anything to George but hey I do love it!

John: You are humble ya know. We love ya and we'll be in the studio above watching from here and seeing ya go on with the show.

We send our love to all listeners and ask them to open their hearts to Murray and you and to know without a doubt, "Oh bla de, O bla da, life goes on RA, la la la la life goes on!"

31

John Lennon's Message on Eternal Opus!
Channeled January 21, 2006

M: John your latest musical creation is brilliant.

Congratulations on Eternal Opus.

J: I'm standing here with ya in case you hadn't noticed me

to your right.

Thank you for your compliments, Marcia. The sound is just

the way I wanted it and as you might have imagined it's about

how we are all eternal, and it's an OPUS to life itself. So

many in your world are misled by religion which teaches so

much untruth, mainly about having to believe in such things

that would only restrict you from knowin that you in fact do go

on, forever! It's a wonderful knowledge they don't want you to

know, so that they can keep blindness over the flock and keep

the donations to their various churches going. It's a scam to

my thinking of course.

M: Oh have I had a hard time with religion and don't I

know it! They condemn our work together. What hogwash! I

*don't know of anyone who would want to bring through
demons or devils in channeling and it's something, which
never crossed my mind. For that matter most of the messages I
have read deal with light and love for mankind, but that is my
vibration of service.*

*J: You are of the service nature to others, never asking for
anything for your great work with Diana. I think it would be
easy to fall prey to using Diana as a way to self-promote and I
have not seen you do that, which is another reason I respect
you so.*

As well, you are basically humble.

*M: But John this was about your new song! Can you share
with me any of the lyrics or the way you did the tune?*

*J: Well what I did was use piano and a good beat to bring
in the feeling for life, and to give our listeners maybe a
different perspective on life, so that they won't have to despair
when they do cross over. As well we are celebrating the debut
of our outlet it means more to me than you may know luv, our*

being able to showcase my work and George's work on your

truly great show, the Forum for World peace!

M: Well John the honor is all mine!

J: Enjoy the song and good luck with tomorrow's show.

Remember peace, remember all you need is love, and I send

on my best wishes.

Bye for now,

Ciao

John

Note: Please refer to Part II Musical Lyrics of this book under the lyrics section to read the song, Eternal Opus.

Wonderful Christmas Time
Channeled, Dec 22, 05

Marcia: Hey John! I'm saying hello to ya. I felt your

presence all around me as I coincidentally heard the song,

'Simply having a Wonderful Christmas time' and other songs.

John: Yeah we were trying to get your attention, as we

want to begin working on the lyrics as soon as possible.

Perhaps today or even tomorrow will work, we know you have

been swamped with work for months and see ya will have a bit

of spare time for this old Beatle.

Marcia: My honor as I have said before. Hey I loved the

website by Graham who was also composing music and lyrics

with you in the 90's. That's pretty cool John. I can't seem to

locate Graham to do a radio show with him or tell him about

our music. Can you say what might have become of Graham?

John: Well no, I can't say what has happened. I do confirm

I was working extensively with Graham and he is also a great

channel. We did some tunes in honor of Yoko and world peace

together; some time ago now, before George crossed over.

35

By the way, George says hello and thanks you for featuring our music every show for your great show the Forum for World Peace. We will be creating more and more for your show, Marcia, through Murray of course. He's a great channel and so are you! We are most happy when we can reach through the veil and forget we're here and perform and play just as we did before crossing, for many years and many tears were shed here in the loneliness and despair of it ya know.

M: Yes John, I well understand. I want to say I liked your short story with meeting up with John Kennedy. I thought the lost pen was a metaphor for me since I have not been writing much of your lyrics, and wish to do some work again.

John; Well actually I had lost my pen, and we had that conversation! And I think that it's true that is a metaphor for the lost lyrics. Just remember Marcia that with the lyrics you are aware that they already exist; and all you have to do is listen, and LOVE. Tune into LOVE and the lyrics will pop into your pretty little head right way without a second thought.

36

M: I hate to admit John that I have lost the titles of the songs and will be on a search to find them before getting back to work.

J: We all lose stuff, it's just part of life. We suggest you check your car, and we are always happy to work with ya at any time! We do think you will be having more time in the New Year and so there is no hurry except that I wanted this stuff out YESTERDAY!

M: Merry Christmas John, I hope you all have a wonderful Christmas on that side, John.

John: Merry Christmas Marcia. We'll be dropping by the studio for drinks and to listen to your show, a group of us will be getting together, Diana included.

Bye for now,

Ciao

John

PS Remember Peace, Remember LOVE is all ya need.

Notes: Please reference the interview with John Lennon and John F. Kennedy, Jr. from Robert Murray from his e-zine titled The Stars Still Shine E-zine, printed in Robert Murray's site, www.thestarsstillshine.com. This is an extraordinary interview with John and JFK, Jr., the special correspondent for the e-zine

John on the Many Splendored Universes
Channeled by Marcia McMahon Feb 3rd, 2007

Hi John. Saying a brief hello. What was that you were saying to me this morning?

John: Hello Marcia my dear. I was saying you don't know how lucky you are waking up in the morning and being in the flesh. It's up to you to realize that truth, as things here are much different. We have our music and our friendships and its wonderful here but the gift of the 3rd dimension, up to the 5th, which is where you are now, is a marvelous thing to behold.

As I stare out at the many splendored universes here from my place, across the universe as it were, I am able to see much more than those on the earth plane.

We do predict that your contacts will be in touch with you soon and a new contract or deal will be set up for you and BBS radio. We want our music out there to give peace a chance, not because of my name, John Lennon or George's name either. We want our talent and music to go on, as it did on this plane. With all the interest in channeling and

39

Ascension many people the world over are turning on to renewed spirituality and to my work from Spirit. Spirit is not an idle place where people strum harps or angels play, no indeed we lads here are busy trying to influence the earth for the better.

We are tired of the antiseptic wars and the horrible suicide bombs and the religion surrounding these tragedies! When will the world wake up to peace and brotherhood?

That's what our message was all about on the earth plane; 'All Ya Need is Love!'

We were speaking of a love of brotherhood and an ideal love, not the romantic love, although we brought that to the fore, too, with my marriage to Yoko.

The Love we wanted to convey was universal love of all! So on that note, we ask you to continue to feature our music on your great show, to showcase it and to persist in the music connections you are making. We wanted this music out yesterday. But we trust in our channels and the wonderful light workers Doug and Don of BBS radio.

Now there is a radio station all about Love!

Luv ya,

John and George of the Half Beats.

Notes: I cannot help but chuckle at the number of times this ex-Beatle references his old songs. "Yesterday" and "All You Need is Love" and so many more references to his great old hits that continue to be played around the world by those who espouse the very meaning of that one, great tune. I saw a Christmas video, circa 2009, on YouTube, done on the theme of "All You need is love" in many countries and I could not but help sense John's divine hand even in that! I am saying that he may have inspired the entire idea and of course his original song inspired it, but the universal appeal of that "All You Need is Love" concept is catching on everywhere some 40 plus years later. It's truly great when it becomes timeless to each generation. That's Shakespeare isn't it! Lennon was the greatest songwriter of the twentieth century.

John: Many Years and Many Tears: The Music for Peace Project
Channeled sometime in 2007

M: John, I'm saying hello to ya.

John: Oh, yeah, we're glad to hear from ya. I see you liked, 'Passing Through Botswana.'

'That's one of George's favorites, and it has a great beat and sound to it.

M: I'm sorry I have not gotten back with more work on the lyrics, and now I've got school coming up and all sorts of things, as well as the next interview with Barry Eaton in Australia.

J: We're very excited for you for that interview. We think that people will get the idea and call the station for more information. I know you are concerned about legal ramifications and ya know I can't advise there; not my forte, ya know.

M: Yeah, but Barry's really into you and your work, John. I hope after all the doubt I must have planted in his mind he'll

42

still do it. I know that there are concerns from Bob Murray and they are justified.

John: Yea to a point. The main reason for my contact with you both is to create the CD and release it to the millions who will have the lyrics in their heads and follow them. The human being tends to operate on remote a lot of the time, as ya know, so this is our contribution to world peace. We hope that you do find an agent, and we've heard about the major publisher being interested in your work with Diana. We applaud that and hope that it's indeed the big break that will make your career! Were' all praying for ya here since the magnitude of your message is truly great.

We want your success just like we want our success. It's been many years and many tears here for me, with loneliness and frustration. We play all the time and record but as I have told ya, there are no producers here to get the word out. Murray's changing all of that with his great musical talents, and we hope you'll have time once the success comes crashing down upon your pretty little head! (laughing)

M: Oh there ya go again teasing me about my pretty little head. I don't have your genius, John. I am merely the channel; creative that I am, I am not on your level, but very honored nonetheless to do this work with you and Diana. I can't express how great the honor truly is, since you were a childhood icon to me. I mean everyone grew up listening to you. I hope your debut from spirit to the world of form has as much impact as the original did, but knowing you in spirit and knowing its true does not a grand entrance make. Once people hear the great tunes I think they'll immediately recognize it's from you. I hope we find the agent to help.

John: Well gotta run for now. We're here for ya and we'll channel in some lyrics whenever you can spare the time. God bless, John

Luv ya.

References: Eaton, B. www.radiooutthere.com Barry is Barry Eaton, a great radio show host and producer in Australia who hosts www.radioutthere.com where I appeared and gave messages from John.

Remember Peace this Christmas
Channeled December 24, 2008

Marcia: Dear John, You're on my mind again and I am wishing to connect to ya.

John: Marcia my dear, how very nice to hear from you. I hope you're having a good Christmastime, as I know you're busy. We're quite busy around here as George and I are always working in the studio. We're glad to see Bob coming up again on your show, as he's a great channel and so are you. We want my music and lyrics out there and into the New Year you'll be getting that break I'm speaking of! It's going to go very big for you and Murray dear so hold on to your hats!

Marcia: John, any word of anyone else you're working with over there?

John: Oh yeah well you know about the big Celebration we had for Diana and George and I really enjoyed entertaining again for that. We have been acting in various skits too and we really enjoy getting out our message to the audiences we have on this side, and wouldn't it be great really if my music could have a label all its own, say with BBS and others who could purchase it online from them? I know many opportunities abound for you and Murray in the New Year so we'll keep going when you have time to channel more lyrics. I know you have felt bad about things not being completed and I ask you not to feel that way. We understand as we are also creative people, and just know when I tell you you're going to be going big.

We'd like to thank Doug and Don Newsome for being the light workers they are and for having faith in Marcia and Bob Murray. We appreciate all the wonderful light work they do for so many by allowing my music and message to go out to the public as it were, and to continue in the creating of Peace for this planet.

Remember Peace this Christmas, Happy New Year and much love always,

John

Notes: John, in his clever way refers to me as "Marcia my dear" and of course it brings up the old Beatles songs and connotations of "Martha My Dear" lyrics to one of the old songs. His words are full of many references to old Beatles tunes.

We Wanted this Out Yesterday: John to Marcia!
Sometime 2006

Marcia: Hi John, I am attempting to connect to you. Are you available?

John: Yeah Marcia we've been waiting to speak to you for days now.

We see you've been corresponding with another of my channels, Chris Moors.

M: Well John they seem to be everywhere! Every time I mention you or our work together I hear from some person or other that they have channeled your vibration in with either music or words. Pretty amazing to me John!

John: Hey yeah, I do resonate with lots of people back on earth. It's my way of saying yeah, we do go on and in my case too, we're creating a lot of rock and roll music on this side, which is being heard by earth—amazing to my mind.

M: Well your mind is brilliant, John. I am still working on the painting a bit stalled due to needing a specific material known as frisket for the completion of the stars, which we cannot do without. I am not able to put them in freehand, at least I don't' think so.

John: Yeah, well it's taking a while Marcia as I see, and, of course, I wanted this out Yesterday. But we never push our channels, as that can be detrimental to the creative process they are in. We've been off the air now for weeks and George and I do have new music for your show. You can ask Murray about how hard I've been working him lately.

M: What are your thoughts on including Christopher in a recording of Murray's work, if Murray were to agree to that? Chris sounds like you John and we could really get it out there for you, John.

John: I'm all for it, Marcia. I would think asking Bob would be the first step and whatever he wants to do is fine. We don't want to get this thing too muddied up with copyright issues as I know you are concerned about that already. Let me see if I've got this straight now, you own the lyrics, Murray of course owns the music and Chris can sing and play just like me?

M: That's about it John.

*John: Well I'd say it's a great idea. But let Murray know first and get with Chris, then on **to** this idea. We can see where it will go. Well got to go now we are in the midst of another recording session on this side with George. We'll send all our loving to you!*

Chow, bye for now,

John

Notes: In this message John references my artwork, which is on the cover of this book, titled John: Across the Universe, original watercolor by Marcia McMahon, M.A.

Inspired by the spirit connection to John that I have, I am a recognized aura painter and painter of Princess Diana and Mother Teresa. I love illustrating my books but have not had time to do more with John's paintings. To buy a copy of the print or view it

Visit www.dianaspeakstotheworld.com and then click Site index. Go to Messages from the Ascended Masters and click Messages from John Lennon. Chris Moors is a former show host with BBS radio who did both Peaceful Planet and Radical Dolphin using my lyrics and Bob's music and both turned out beautifully. I feel such thanks and gratitude to Chris Moors, although I cannot locate him presently.

Give Peace a Chance on the Peaceful Planet Show
Channeled, July 2006

Marcia: Hi John, I'm hearing ya.

John: Yeah Marcia. Long time no channeling babe! We're glad to see you're back up and live with our music on your show. And congratulations on the new person who will be helping with the music. We're delighted to see this great stuff finally be moved to the mass consciousness, as I had predicted it would.

All we are saying is give peace a chance and that is what this show is all about.

Diana sends her love and we are all gathered now in the upstairs studio as we over-light your program and hear your work live.

WE love ya, yeah, yeah, yeah, from this old Beatle with love

John

52

Notes: BBS radio underwent some management changes for a time and cancelled the show. This was not due to popular demand but someone had briefly been allowed to take overall management decisions. So when they terminated him a month later, Carolyn Evers, a dear friend and light worker well known on BBS radio, called me with an offer to appear on her show. I did and the show was back on air. You cannot imagine how personally John took this change and vowed to help me get back on air. I found out the world of Internet radio is one of constant competition and change. It's a lot of work to round up great guests each week, review their books, and be articulate in every instance in addition to bringing in readings with Spirit and the angels and feature the music; all in one short hour a week. We always had a packed show and many listeners; but I never got an offer to do anything with the music as John predicted so many times. John said he could not advise me legally but that when Yoko heard of my work she would be all for the peace he is trying to create on the earth plane through music. I personally know our connection to John is genuine, there have been way too many confirmations for me to doubt; and frankly how is it that Bob Murray "gets" the music and I get the lyrics? Was that all coincidence or what?

Photo by Sherri White, Beatles fan Sherri, taken August 11, 2006. Sherri told me this was taken in New York at Strawberry Fields Memorial in Central Park. I love the Sunflower on the mosaic of Imagine- very powerful and it goes with this next message. (White, S. 2009)
www.myspace.com/sunflowersherry

Strawberry Fields Remembrance – 25 Years after John

As I watched the thousands gather at Strawberry Fields in Central Park, via television the evening of John's anniversary of his tragic death some 25 years earlier, his image began to form in my living room. Suddenly, John stood before me, open faced, smiling and keen to give a heartwarming message to his fans from all over the world.

I felt the strongest presence I ever had in my years of medium ship, and he even gave me the mental impression of how wonderful he looked and felt that evening. He was strong and handsome, clean-shaven with shorter hair that he is remembered for. Here is John's message to his fans. My eyes, which were tear filled, dried up and I felt the most wonderful presence of unconditional love. Whenever I channel John I connect to his loving vibration. He really was the world's most sincere troubadour of love.

John's 25th Anniversary Message to His Fans
Channeled by Marcia McMahon December 8, 2006

John: Hey, yeah, it's me, John. I'm showing' ya how I look now; you see, no scars, no fear. My hair is shorter and I'm clean-shaven!

I do look every bit myself, but in spirit, not in form. We're quite excited to be on your show, Marcia. Don't worry too much about Yoko she's all for world peace and when she does hear from ya, you know she's gonna luv ya! We wish to say thanks to all my fans and for all the good times! We want to ask people to open their hearts to Bob Murray's music- and to say that it is really mine through Bob, and to say your lyrics are mine through you! Your lyrics were good but not complete! We hope to do more with you to Rock and Roll the Beatles once again!

IMAGINE PEACE

IMAGINE LOVE

Soon your world will eventually get this message and we'll all be on our way to ascension!

Ciao,

John

John Lennon: Love Around the World. ©Original

watercolor by Marcia McMahon

Inspired by John

©. 2006 prints available from Ascended Masters Art site by Marcia

http://www.angelfire.com/mb2/diana_speaks/ascendedmas tersart.html

John inspired this portrait to capture some of the old Beatles feeling of love, including the rainbow portrait and the big world in his heart chakra. This is what John accomplished on the Earth plane as a Beatle- to bring love around the world to millions.

Wouldn't it be wonderful to bring our music and lyrics that John is inspiring us to write to the world again and let John's spirit guide our world to peace. Imagine! John intends that and it's up to the world to hear it.

John on Possibilities for the New Year
Channeled December 2006

Marcia: Hey John I am saying hello to ya. I've meant to do more with your work, and yet I seem to find time to do many other things. Sorry dear.

John: Marcia, my dear, John, here, coming in loud and clear. Hey, we understand you are a creative and busy person, doing all you can to bring awareness and ascension to all. We know how hard you work to do your show, and your other channeling with other ascended masters and Archangels.

M: How are things on the other side these days?

J: These days rather busy as usual. George and I are always in the studio, another year has come and gone with scarcely noticed it. We are glad to see you make new connections for an agent, that is just what you need darling. We've been saying all along that a good agent will help get the word out and let the world know what we're doing with music with Murray on this side, as well as the lyrics. There are others of my channels throughout the world who also *deserve a break, and many will be coming to your show in the New Yea, Marcia **my** dear. As well, we want your work with Diana out there as it's very important, and she continues her important work on this side with the children of aids.*

M; Yes I well imagine, John. I am signing off, but thanks again for the update John.

J: Anytime we have a spare minute my thoughts do drift in of you. You are a wonderful peace worker and light worker and it's a great honor to work with you my dear.

Remember peace, Remember love!

With love from John,

John

Notes: Esther Goldberg, aka Queen Ladybug has appeared on my show a number of times and is a most talented musician from Manchester, England. She feels a spiritual connection to John Lennon and her music is written in an inspired fashion to Bob Murray's music. I hosted her on two shows in which she sang, "Here I Am," and a few others of her hits. She is self-taught and a powerhouse of talent. John's predictions came true once again. Remember, that in the spirit world, predictions do take time to materialize, as Spirit is beyond time in the normal linear sense that we know it. So I hope that John is correct about his music going big once more, and that I can assist in some way with the project on a continuing basis. We haven't yet got all the pieces of the game arranged, but I am waiting on spirit and doing my part. Goldberg, E. www.myspace.com/queenladybug

John's Music for Peace
October, 14, 2006

M: John, saying hello to you. Sorry it's been a while and I have had such inertia on the project. I do care about you and the music, as you know.

J: Oh yeah, well we were wondering when you might make contact since you have been avoiding us or so it seemed.

M: Not at all John just a lot of other things happening and a lack of desire to be on the computer day and night I have not abandoned you or the progress of the music and lyrics.

J: I know I am giving you a twist Marcia dear; knowing how you feel at times it can be hard to be motivated adequately when it seems the world is not noticing your wonderful work for peace or Diana's; much less George and I. Believe me when I tell you that you are going big very soon and an offer will be forthcoming for your lyrics, Bob's music and a deal of some sort for BBS radio. I can't divulge all of it because I can't say I know who will be helping ya, but just trust me, as I know you do Marcia my dear.

Marcia: John; Every time you predict something it does come true; even more so that others who have said thus and so. You are usually right on. How is the music on the other side with George doing these days?

John: Oh George says he loves your work and your show by the way and we're always working on more tunes for Murray to channel in. He is always on a lot of projects like you are so sometimes it's hard to get a hold of him too. We are playing for the club, now and then, with Michael and the Band. We are also involved in some other creative outlets.

We want to get the music out to earth and do all we can for peace and bring the people to the awareness of peace thru my name.

Well, we are in session now and got to run.

Luv ya babe!

Ciao,

John

Notes: We did not get a contract for our music on the BBS network. It has not yet materialized due to a number of issues. We are hesitant in proceeding to widely distribute lyrics or songs although we do own the copyright on all of our lyrics and music. We feel it's best to let the opportunity come to us the right way. We are waiting for the right opportunity to use Bob's inspired music and my lyrics to bring them to the fore. It has to be done with the greatest care with respect to the huge name the Beatles, and of course John's former family.

The Half Beats in the New Year!
Channeled by Marcia McMahon, Dec 2007

M: Dear George and John, I am feeling like maybe one of you will want to speak this morning about the up and coming developments for the New Year.

J: Well Marcia my dear as you have known all along you, Murray and BBS will be getting into a new venture with our music from heaven. We're all so glad for you and are waiting with baited breath here, to see how it all develops into a deal or contract of some sort.

We want our music out to the rest of the world because it will again affect the whole planet the way it did originally with the impact of the Beatles. Only as you know now, we're calling our new group the Half Beats! We think it's a great play on words and, of course, that was all my idea! We have been playing gigs here for the Opera house, and we also work with Michael and the Band, all through Bob Murray's great talent.

J: We ask you to further your pursuits with the agent and the contact she gave you and leave no stone unturned until you find someone who will represent you and the boys at BBS in their wonderful efforts to get all their music out.

We want you to give Don a call this week to discuss it. We're looking after you and all people on the planet to give you the best chance for Peace yet! The year 2007 can be a pivotal year for peace if the people will take back their power and demand it!

We congratulate you personally, Marcia, on all your new projects and while we wish we had time to do more with the lyrics you will be doing that as well. So don't forget to set aside for channeling. Also we'd like to suggest our listeners visit Bob's site and download some of our latest tunes.

All the best and I send "All my loving" to you Marcia and all your listeners!

Happy New Year! Remember Peace, remember love!

John

Notes: Bob Murray's site is located at
www.thestarstillshine.com, where you can listen to the
inspired music for free or a small download fee.
http://www.TheStarsStillShine.com/musicbuy.html

John: http://www.thestarsstillshine.com/musicbuy.html

George: http://www.thestarsstillshine.com/musicbuy.html

Up Late in the Studio with George
Channeled Jan 2007

M: Good Morning John. My sincerest apologies for not speaking in so long John, but here I am.

J: Hi Marcia dear, you're coming in loud and clear here. Sorry I have not been up long as we had a sort of all-night gigs with George in the studio working on some new tunes. I am a bit foggy. Can we speak a bit later on, then, this afternoon?

M: Hi John, I'm back and are you feeling a bit better now?

J: Yeah I am thanking you, Marcia my dear. Many people think we do not have time here, but we do and we also sleep. I appreciate the kindness of your waiting for me.

M: Well John I wanted to ask your opinion on what else you might suggest to get the music going? I have the new power point, which is simple, and easy to read, maybe it does not say it all, but it is a start for promotional tools.

J: Marcia everything you do looks good to me. I like it. It should help. I would suggest music be in it, as well, what about The Fest for Beatle Fans?

M: My next question, is it worth my time and effort since it is not New Age but so mainstream? Usually with channeling- the mainstream people take great offense when someone says they're channeling someone famous.

John: Yeah, I know all about the trouble most of my channels have had. Darn shame. People are waking up all over the world with the ascension movement and we the Beatles started it. We began the Love Generation. I've talked about that before in our many messages but for once I think people simply have to understand this is John Lennon speaking here and this is not some deluded person making it up.

I have spoken of all that, all the same issues that were important in my life as John and written many love songs for Yoko. I would think that would be enough. Surf the website first and make up your own mind about going up there. Have you tried to reach Yoko or my former family? I know that is really risky business but they are the ones with all the power and money to do this for you and BBS.

We also like the idea of the power point. Work on that today and ask Don to send it on to the list for you. It should catch some eyes. Well George and I were up last night working in the studio on some new tunes that Bob will be channeling in soon. We'll let you go for now.

Ciao. This is John here and I send all my loving to you and my former fans.

With love from John.

John: Listen to Blackbird!
Channeled sometime in 2006

M: Hello John, I am curious about Ladybug Claudine and our new connection together and with you.

J: Yeah, I am very excited about your meeting up with another great light worker like yourself, Claudine.

M: Can you clarify what you meant John in her reference to Blackbird being played on a recorder?

J: Marcia my dear, you will have to seek that song out and see what it does when you hear it. I know I'm being a bit cryptic but you will get the meaning of it all when you do a bit of homework from this old Beatle.

By the way we are all quite pleased about Bob's new CD, Dead on the Ed Sullivan Show. Ed is producing us once again in heaven and everybody here is quite excited about our new style of songwriting and performances with the show.

We can't wait to share this with your listening audience all in the name of Peace and love of course and not because of my fame or name. That is all behind me now although those of earth will recognize my style as well as George's style that has greatly evolved.

We are both glad to be working together on the same goals for the Peaceful Planet.

We have all the lyrics and while you're off next week we hope to channel some of the new lyrics into the earth plane through you.

We are quite excited about Claudine's talent being aired on your show and see a possible collaboration of sorts with my music and yours, with Bob Murray's permission given first. Right now I know you have a lot going on and we'll leave you to ponder the delights of spirit and the many wonders you do work for your audience as well.

With love from John,

The Half Beats John and George.

PS: Remember peace, remember love!

Notes: Bob Murray of www.thestarstillshine.com produced an album available only online called, Dead on the Ed Sullivan Show. All Rights reserved, Robert Murray. I highly recommend it! Our show airs parts of the new CD as we can.

Excerpt from our show: This was part of an ad airing on the BBS network at that time.

You were listening to Peaceful planet synthesized from spirit thru the medium-ship of Robert Murray, online at www.thestarsstilshine.com

Check out our ascension series interviews with world teachers as we all strive here on BBS to bring Peace to our Planet.

When I finally did hear Blackbird I realized a very personal message from John about myself. That's all I can say but it hit me fairly strongly and it was right on.

A New Earth Is Being Born; John's Thoughts on Ascension

Channeled summer 2007

M: Hello John. I am sensing you, or feeling your good vibration.

John: Marcia my dear, long time no channeling Babe. We ask you to set aside at least a half hour a day to write Dead on Ed Sullivan Show. We see a big contract coming your way and Murray's way. We hope it will bring you the success you both rightly deserve.

M: Oh, John. I've been meaning to ask you about Ascension, and spiritual progress if I may.

John: Yeah I was trying to reach you my dear Marcia. There is nothing to fear about Ascension, as it's really all about love and unfolding.

M: Well I had read the <u>Sirian Revelations</u> saying that our New Earth would be only be etheric. The Sirians said Planet

Earth would be absorbed into the Sun in 2012, just four years from now!

John: Marcia my dear you are taking all of this quite seriously and we want to assure you that entering into the new vibration of the New Earth will be perceived as gentle a process as possible.

You will meet up with Princess Diana, and all of us, and all will become One on the Peaceful Plane, living as one in a blissful New Earth. The New Earth is being born right from within each one of us. It's hard to describe or know it completely until we all live it!

Until then live as ONE in peace and love and fear not. We will be right here for you should you ever need us. Just call and I'll be there.

In peace and Love

Your friend,

John Lennon.

References: Corri, P. C. 2006 www.SirianRevelations.com retrieved July 2009

Notes: Her trilogy is channeled from the Sirian High Council that is to say the star system Sirius not the radio station, on what they believe will occur on planet earth in the year 2012. If you read channeling as you are doing here she is well worth the read even if you don't buy it.

Much has been said in other chapters where I devote time to understanding the phenomena of Ascension, which is a cosmic occurrence to our Solar System and is spoken of with great anticipation by John. Archangel Michael's messages clarify somewhat the divine nature of the occurrence, and each is of course free to believe what they want to believe.

The New Earth is collectively known in Ascension or New Age circles as a fifth dimensional Earth that is possibly more etheric, and hence referenced as the New Earth.

I have channeled information about the New Earth. It's a big deal and no one in mainstream media will touch it; the end of the world as we know it—naturally gives us pause for concern.

However a New Earth is being born as John reassures us in his message and lyrics- and we have only to wait to see this Golden Age manifest. I personally have an opinion on the New Earth given to me by my highest Angel guides. There is nothing to fear in entering the fifth dimension unless you are permanently stuck in the third dimensional consciousness of limitation, lack, guilt and fear. My angels tell me that all of that will be a thing of the past as we fully realize our Christ Consciousness and ascend with the planet into the fifth dimension. It is designed to be a rare opportunity for all of us. I am not so sure I want the world to end; but I at least understand this to be a consciousness event of great love and unity unlike anything ever experienced before.

However, I predict when the great earth changes begin to occur mankind will have a mass awakening. This event is unlike anything else experienced by earth before, and many will realize that it is not just a consciousness-expanding event like the 60's were. Instead, this awakening to love will signal a cosmic and physical event unparalleled in comparison to anything we have yet experienced on the planet.

My work with Archangel Michael highlights many aspects of Ascension in a beautiful and informative way and it dovetails nicely with what John has said about us moving up to the fourth or fifth dimension. Surely with all the information about 2012 and Ascension on the Internet there could not be a New Age conspiracy to create Ascension scenarios! The Age of Aquarius is supposed to be a golden age of equality, trust and love. The purpose of any channeling is to bring forth otherwise unavailable information that is important for the people of the earth plane.

In this case John's music and words as well as those of AA Michael inform us of something changing on the Earth; and we should inform ourselves! Therefore, while I do digress I want the readers to do their own investigation of the Ascension movement and to educate themselves to this as much as possible before 2012, which is now only three years away.

I am ever grateful to John for his thoughts about ascension and his confidence that all will be well. He apparently has seen it from the other side.

Notes: **Ascension Teachings with Archangel Michael**. By Marcia McMahon, Published 2012, available on Amazon.com or on the website at www.angelfire.com/mb2/diana_speaks/ArchangelMichaelsMessags.html

John: Across the Universe to Polaris
Channeled Feb 2, 2008

M: Hey John: I've been thinking of you with all the news and press about the song, "Across the Universe" being projected to the star system called Polaris.

J: Oh yeah, it's a really big deal for NASA. Too bad they will not talk about the work they are all doing with extraterrestrial life on other planets in our solar system.

I am pleased that not only I but also Paul have gone global and Across the Universe!

Those were my words, Marcia my dear. I would ask your listeners and guests to hear the great tunes Bob Murray is doing thru your work and to play some of the music today. Remarkable Nebulae would be a great one to feature and be sure to read your lyrics. Of course the other version of it is Remarkable Diana.

We the Half Beats, George and John are pleased to see what is being done to save the Planet for unity consciousness

79

and peace. We ask all to give peace a chance and to give our great music from the other side the chance it deserves so that people everywhere can turn on to peace as they did when I was on the earth plane.

This is John Lennon here saying hello to all our fans out there, Across the Universe!

Luv ya,

Ciao

John.

Notes: In 2008 NASA launched a space beam to Polaris the brightest star in our galaxy and sent the lyrics of, 'Across the Universe,' out there to other possible star systems via radio waves!

Notes: Friedman, S. retrieved 2006, www.stantonfriedman.com one of my most stunning interviews was with the famous author Stan Friedman; a UFO expert, who has written volumes about Roswell and then the Betty and Barney Hill case. John is informing us of something grander here if you accept the message at face value. In my experience there is plenty of evidence of this phenomenon.

References: NASA. www.nasa.gov

John Speaks on Ringo's 68th birthday!
Channeled by Marcia, 2007

Marcia: Saying hello to you John.

John: Yeah, Babe, long time no channeling. I hope things are going well as I know that there is a lot of change coming your way these days.

M: Yeah an interview with Barry and then with our radio show tomorrow. I was wondering what you thought about the Ringo Starr celebration on Larry King show and on Yoko's appearance on TV?

J: Oh yeah well we're glad to see Ringo turn another year around the Sun. We're all very proud of Ringo's accomplishments ya know. As well, it was great seeing Yoko live on TV, in her white hat. It has become somewhat of a trademark. I am all for the revival of Peace and Love. As you know we all stood up for that back then and now at this time on the planet, we are finally seeing the masses of people stand up and do something for peace and love.

81

M: Yeah I thought it was a great interview with Ringo and he looks wonderful for 68. Wouldn't you be about 64 now John? It makes me think of the song "When I'm 64." It was a great tune, but I for one, among many, am sorry you did not get there.

John: Yeah well that's all history now and I want my fans to know that I am still doing this great music with Bob Murray from the other side and your lyrics to go with the music will be available via your show the Peaceful planet.

We are Is creating more music and lyrics when you do have time and we'd love to see the book out soon, but I know you are held up by things in your personal life at the moment and that involves a lot of change for you. So just keep a smile on your face and don't let anything get you down you know. We wish you all the best and want to thank Barry for his interest in our great music.

Ciao for now,

Luv ya,

John

Channeling and Free Will Choice

Excerpted Article by Lady Isis

"Channeling"

The word channel says it all:

Channel: n. groove, tube, passage, conduit, canal. v. convey, conduct, direct, steer, lead, funnel.

Channeling: to send through. Any information coming from 'beyond' this dimension is channeled information, whether it is done in automatic writing, telepathic transformation (conscious channeling) or medium-ship, which is the allowing of another spirit to use your body as a host to speak. The medium through "freewill choice" steps aside and allows a spirit to come in and consciously does not know what is being said until they are told after coming back into full consciousness. This practice is only dangerous if one does not use the proper protection, which one should use even in daily living in this day and age of dimensional changes and blending. Nothing or no one cannot attack, take us over, nor do anything to you that you do not invite by a choice you have made, either during or before incarnation.

Strangely enough, medium-ship and freewill choice is one subject I can speak about from vast experience. On many occasions, I have been the spirit, "allowed" to come in and use a host body to speak. And I know I had to have "permission" from the owner of that body in order to do so. One such time was when I as the one speaking through The Delphic Oracle.

———————

Freewill Choice: Freewill choice is never taken away. It is impossible to do so. Do you think the Creator would take away from you something He/She has given? Absolutely not! It must be "given away" by you, by a freewill choice you make. That is why there are no victims, only volunteers in life. You make choices every split second of your life, and each of those choices bears fruit. "You reap what you sow."

In the Light of the ONE,

Lady Isis

Isis, L. *

http://groups.yahoo.com/group/TheLightCircleEzine/ *

Retrieved Nov 09 from the E-zine.

* Read my Consciousness Raising Magazine and Monthly Messages from Matthew *

* Published Worldwide 365 days a year since 2-22-02 * by Isis "Lady of the Light"

* http://groups.yahoo.com/group/TheLightCircleEzine/ *

* Subscribe: TheLightCircleEzine-subscribe@yahoogroups.com *

Notes: I included this excerpt from the Circle of Light E-zine in which I am regularly published with my messages from spirit. In particular many of John's messages are published there. Lady Isis is a pseudonym for her name. However she feels a connection to the goddess Isis.

What is channeling, and what is the difference between a channel and a medium? That is a topic that is deserving of merit, since many people assume that a channel does exactly what a medium does. Not so! I am myself more of a channel than a medium, a channel is a special person with a gift of being able to receive words from the spirit exactly as they speak or write them thru the person, whereas a medium brings thru the essence of a message in their own words from a spirit on the other side. I do differ with Lady Isis a bit since I feel channeling is different from medium-ship. I agree with Lady Isis on the point of a medium, a so-called voice medium that is a direct voice for the deceased as the deceased speaks thru the direct voice channel or medium. Confusing? Yes I know but there are different gifts and it's important in the chronology of this book to understand my work with John Lennon. I am a channel for John Lennon, Princess Diana, Archangel Michael, Mother Mary, Jeshua and many of the spiritual hierarchy. I am also a medium; in that I do bring through messages from ancestors, but it's not my specialty! My specialty is to be a conduit for the masters and talent in the etheric realms to convey their special messages to humanity, rather than a specific person. Usually this takes the form of books or articles; so I am a scribe more so than medium. But the gift's distinctions are very subtle. For those who have never heard from spirit this can be confusing, but let me explain further.

A medium like John Edward brings in relatives, conditions of death, and proof of the continuity of all life. The deceased family loved ones are all around a medium and that is their specialty. A channel is a person who is conduit of a master, a teacher or higher evolved being, ascended master or archangel. They tend to bring through what we call an Ascended Master, who has a strong purpose for teaching or message in reaching a wider audience than just the immediate family; and they are speaking on topics of importance to all humanity. So a channel tends to impart wisdom, while a medium will bring in a message from Aunt Mildred. Is there a difference? Only if you believe that Archangel Michael has something more important to say than Aunt Mildred. But the caveat is that it is relative sometimes to the recipient!

While John says he does not want to be regarded as an Ascended Master, he does say that he works with a number of enlightened souls on the earth plane. In that he gives us a glimpse into his mission and vision of a peaceful planet, I personally believe he is an Ascended Master. But whatever the terminology of that; he is doing work for humanity, for peace.

He was an advanced soul who stood for peace on the earth plane whilst here. His messages, through me, sound identical to the living John Lennon and therefore I am convinced it is he speaking through me. As I always say, though, believe what you want to believe.

I am both channel and medium, but my books are channeled.

While I am sure I could bring through messages for Yoko and his former family I have never contacted them openly, out of respect for their privacy. If they were to approach me after completing the book I would certainly be willing to help. It's not my job, as a channel, to work with the relatives of those whom I channel; though I was asked, by Princess Diana, to post my messages to Prince William and Harry on my site, www.dianaspeakstotheworld.com. I certainly obliged her in that. However I am not in any way trying to reach the House of Windsor or Yoko to let either of them know of my spirit contact. That may be, in time, in spirit's own way. Whilst I do wish her well, as I do all of Diana's family, it would seem intrusive for me to contact any of them.

I am perfectly able to be a medium and have functioned as such for many of my readings; as I do sense the presence of loved ones for those with whom I do readings. My true love is being a scribe and a writer, so that I can be the pen of some of the greatest of the world's talent and sages and modern day Ascended Masters, such as Princes Diana.

If you think I could ever make up these statements from John, then you are giving me a great deal of credit! I am a creative person but not that CREATIVE! You have not yet even seen the half of the lyrics John has given me, either. I believe what sets my work apart from medium-ship is the number of books I have written inspired by the spirits of the very talented and gifted souls now departed.

Dear Reader, I hope you begin to understand the subtle differences between mediums and channels, they are important to the next event that was to unfold in my work with John and those who knew him as an early Beatle!

Meeting the Pete Best Band, Rend Lake, Illinois 2008

One of the most amazing events to take place in my work with John was coincidentally meeting up with the Pete Best Band in Rend Lake Resort, Illinois, while they were on tour for a George Harrison day's festival.

My husband and I arrived for dinner that evening and set up camp prior to stopping by Rend Lake Lodge and Restaurant. We arrived in time for a delicious fish dinner on Friday night. Afterwards, we thought we'd step out onto a deck overlooking Rend Lake since the evening was so warm and lovely. As we stepped outside to the deck area, I heard thick Liverpool accents at a table of musicians. They were scheduled to play on the agenda for the Harrison Fest tomorrow! George Harrison Days were being held in Benton, IL, in the fall of 2008. It had to be them. I could sense my heart beating now in my chest more heavily.

I could sense and feel John's spirit standing right beside me that night amongst the Band members on the deck, overlooking the lake that evening. As sure as could be, I had stepped right into the inner circle of the Pete Best Band! I pondered the question how to convey that to them? Hum... I knew I had to speak up about my work but was nervous suddenly. I began to think how approach the lads from

England who all were drinking heavily. I said, "Hi, you must be the Pete Best Band!" They said, "Yeah, we are!" And then began a most interesting evening.

Phil who sat next to me began by telling me that they still lived in the Casbah; the original hangout of the original Beatles back in Liverpool! We chatted casually until I began to reveal that I had a radio show which was featuring the music inspired by Bob Murray with both John Lennon and George Harrison from the other side. They were keen to know more about my medium-ship and I sensed extreme cynicism from some of the members. Someone immediately began to accuse me of trying to make a living off John's legacy! This was quite the opposite since I have never made a dime on my musical project with John or my book as yet still unpublished. They did not realize of course that I had not set out to make money on the project. But Pete Best was a former Beatle after all and he had rights to this musical Beatles revival type band and must have worked out the rights with the other living Beatles such as Ringo, Paul and Yoko. So I did not begrudge them their work at all.

According to the Beatle's history, Pete Best was the very first drummer before Ringo arrived on the scene. Pete was known for his good looks and talent, but not everyone was happy with Pete in the original Beatles group. It was said that he was anti-social with the rest of the Beatles- again not my opinion but that of Wikipedia, when they performed in Hamburg before they became big. By the time they returned to England its thought that Pete had been replaced with the advice of George Martin, a new manager, and Ringo took his place. Pete was gifted with many talents and went into public service in England. Pete was a scholar and an A student and the rest of the Beatles really weren't gifted academically, although I feel John was a genius that slipped through the system there due to his other interests. He could have been extremely gifted academically given his brilliant mind.

As the night wore on they wanted me to provide proof of my connection to family members in spirit; but did not seem interested at all in messages from John and George. This struck me curious since that's how I introduced myself - as a channel for the spirit of John Lennon! (Channel vs. medium; round one!)

I gladly obliged by trying to explain the difference between a channel and medium. "A medium is a person who brings through messages for others to confirm the continuity of life and those messages are brief and from family members. A channel, on the other hand, is a person who has a mission from spirit, from the other side, and is often writing through the voice or pen of the person wanting the messages brought forth. Hence this one is able to write using a pen that is actually in the speaking style and mannerisms of voice that the deceased used in life, as proof of life after death. There are even full voice channels that channel the voice of the deceased thru their voice and you can even hear the voice."

None of the members of the Best Band ever seemed to grasp the definition that I attempted to explain. Instead they wanted me to bring in their family members! (Channel vs. medium round two!)

The spirit of the great John Lennon stood there among us waiting to be allowed to speak through me, and they seemed to want family members instead. I have to think of the irony of that. John wanted to be heard and I had to honor his request. I am a medium, but more so a channel. That really confused them for some reason since they apparently never met a channel or a medium so that they could not tell the difference; and it is subtle. I did not give up trying to convey John's thoughts that evening though. This began to unfold when I was asked by Pete to bring in a message from John. He sat at the opposite end of the table, sipping silently away at his beer and looking rather stoic.

Suddenly, a cool breeze caused the chills to run through me as the coldness of the night settled on my shoulders. Unfortunately, I did not have adequate protection from the cold and the chills came over me. It was doubly embarrassing! I am a bit of a nervous Nellie as John would say, but either it was the cold night air or the channeling for Pete that brought on sudden nerves. I was shaking uncontrollably! Darn- I thought, just what I didn't need now!

I had appeared on many radio and TV shows channeling John, before; so I did think it was the chilly night air. Then to my relief, John became to form his thoughts in my mind.

John's Message to Pete Best

John: Yah know, Pete, that I never thought you got the fair end of the deal. I mean George [Martin] simply made that choice for us and we weren't given any alternatives. But I thought that you got a raw deal and did not think you were well treated. I, for one, felt it was a mistake; but anyway there it is and I've said it—what I wanted to say to you over all these forty some years, or more.

I'm glad to see you back out playing in our name and I'd like to ask you to consider doing our music with Marcia's lyrics and Bob Murray's music. Just ask her to show you the lyrics. We do go on and we're creating great music on this side. I'm asking you to consider the offer.

Pete sat there unmoved by all of this; smiled slightly and took another sip out of the beer bottle. He had a stoic personality and I was not the first person to realize this, from what I've read. So I had a hard time understanding his reaction; it seemed to me like he never heard a word of John. Maybe it's that I am a gentle and not a forceful channel. I don't use a bullhorn to blast my messages once I get the stage; nor am I arrogant as a person. There are some loud, overbearing obnoxious medium types out there who make a noisy show, for them to get attention. That's just not my style. I felt ok that he had no reaction; as that seemed to be his style. He was still thinking over what John said.

Feeling awkward, I moved into another position and began to speak with the other young men of the band, named Phil and Roag. Phil was quite a nice person and really opened up to this and so did Roag. Both began to tell me of their home in Liverpool and the Beatles' history. This was due to the fact that their mother, Mona ran this place called the Casbah back in the 60's and they still lived there. I couldn't have been happier hearing this from Phil and Roag; wow, perfect timing for a Beatles history lesson! I thought, "This is so cool—getting to speak with people who still lived there and played where the once unknown Beatles played! What a thrill it was! Whether or not the Best Band accepted my work with John on behalf of peace, I was still so thrilled to meet them all and hear about Liverpool and the old Beatles haunts.

Roag spoke up and asked for a reading. I was not sure at that time of his actual name it was something that escaped me. I located his vibration, which was all I needed for John.

Roag asked, "Does John remember my father?" That was the question.

I said, *"John is saying 'Yes, of course he remembers your father!'"*

Roag smiled and was quietly interested. Then he asked, "What about my mother?" I said I did not get anything right away. Later I found out that Mona had an affair with Phil Aspinall and Roag was the son of this union.

Phil went on to tell us more about living at the Casbah and how cool it was. He did not ask for a reading but seemed genuinely curious about my music and lyrics. So off I went to the truck, and came back with the printed version of some of them. We were looking at Peaceful Planet and Radical Dolphin lyrics. I read them aloud. Some of the guys in the band kept ordering more drinks and it was becoming clear to me that they were really getting inebriated.

I invited Roag to bring the band on my show to help promote their new album and he genuinely wanted to appear on my show to help their CD release. But then, someone else asked me to bring thru a relative. John immediately spoke up and said to tell him "I don't' like the fact that you are testing my channel!" John was defensive and I sensed trouble here, somehow, but was truly trying to help this young man locate a loved one. Somehow I got nothing. Strange, I thought, since many of the loved ones do make themselves known or I see them. At that point I decided to gather up my many pages of lyrics and dismiss myself. The night had worn on and the novelty had worn off. They were talking about other things.

I learned that, while spirit can and does arrange many coincidences for us, it's up to each of us how we choose to respond to spirit's intervention and invitation to believe. Not all in the Pete Best band, including perhaps Pete, were at all interested in my music or lyrics from the other side. Did Pete recognize John's voice in the message about being fired from the Beatles by George Martin? I feel he heard John through my message; but I'll never know. I know that John wrote this material through me because of the constant correspondence I had and confirmations from Bob Murray and many others who have a spirit connection to John. Spirit had arranged the entire meeting, as John confirmed later to me. It was not as well received by some of the members of the Pete Best Band. John had a message later the next day to say about it. I saw the band the next day, milling about a music shop in Benton IL, by some strange coincidence. By then, I was too shy to deliver it at all. I was not sure it would change one thing about their attitude and yet it was so very true!

Maybe one day I'll get to meet Paul McCartney or Ringo Star, what a thrill that would be!

I understand Paul had an experience like this with a blues musician who seemed to bring through some of John's music with him. I am sorry I cannot recall his name. I did have a dream, once, in which I met Paul. In the dream I brought thru messages from both John Lennon and Princess Diana. I also greatly admire Paul's talent. Wouldn't it be wonderful if the living Beatles found a positive interest in the lyrics? But they are so big; I would be the last person to ask them if they were interested. John would be pleased though.

References: **Wikipedia,
http://en.wikipedia.org/wiki/Pete_Best**

Pete Best Band History, retrieved Feb 6, 2010

John's Message to the Pete Best Band
Channeled October 12, 2008 Rend Lake, IL

Marcia: Hi John. Thank you so much for coming thru for Pete, Phil and the others in the Pete Best band.

John: You're welcome. You see I told you I was there among you last night. One would have agreed, if even the greatest skeptic, if that were pure coincidence or not?

I led you to that moment. While not all were satisfied, I have something to say to the one who harassed my channel—she is my channel and she does in fact work with George and me! I don't like the attitude and she doesn't do readings with Aunt Mildred!

As to Phil and the other person Roag, who asked for a reading, there is a "son" of the band that asked about his mum and dad. Yes he is a sort of family relation, though the father never admitted it. He was our producer. We were all aware of it, yeah.

So my message to the boys in the Pete Best band is to remember what we stood for then: Peace and Love! And George asks that you consider the offer my channel is giving ya. We wanted the music out yesterday and it will become a Peaceful Planet. Do your part for peace and love before it's too late.

Luv ya,

Ciao,

John

References: http://en.wikipedia.org/wiki/Pete_Best Retrieved Feb 6, 2010. www.wikpedia.com has a section on the Pete Best band and I checked it after I channeled this message from John about the band. Interesting, all of it was right on! I had no clue who Roag Best was. Roag is the son of Pete Aspinall, a manager for the early Beatles. So my confirmations were there all along, if they had "Ears to hear with, and eyes to see with," as the Master used to say.

John's Message to Roag Best

Perhaps now you get a sense of the urgency of John's drive for peace, as he does not give up on his musical projects. He has left no stone unturned and I cannot reveal how many people I know through the show that he has made offers to, concerning the music. He has had so much success in his music on the earth plane—due to his drive when he was living—to let setbacks and attitudes drive him away from his passion now in the heavenly realms. Even now, in the heavenly realms he still wants to imagine a better world and dream big for the children of earth. "Imagine" still goes on, as does life on the spirit planes. Being a channel for John is a great honor but also requires my faith and courage to keep going despite setbacks. Roag, as I said is in fact the son of Aspinall and that's documented in various sources, Wikipedia for one. (Pete Best History, Wikipedia,) So everything I brought through for them was accurate and right on, at George Harrison days in Benton, IL

The show the Pete Best Band put on was well done and sounded just like the old Beatles as we knew and loved them growing up. The feeling generated in the crowd was great, the "All You Need is Love" freedom that inspired the original Beatles. They honored Bob Bartell, the local Illinois man, known as "Beatle Bob", who saved George Harrison's sister's home from demolition It is now a historical landmark and bed and breakfast in Benton IL. I even did a message for one of the owners of that Bed and Breakfast, called a "Hard Day's Night" while being part of the festival. I was still thrilled to hear them play and channel John Lennon for them. My job as a channel is simply to "show up" and be there. John was right about everything said in the channeled messages to the Best Band and all his information for instance about Roag being a son of the band turned out to be right on! No one can tell me that was a coincidence and I feel John planned it that way. John, as well, told me he loved the old time Beatles tunes and the feeling generated in the crowd with the Pete Best Band. I think it was his sense of wanting that back somehow. Some of the members of the Pete Best Band were perfectly astonished!

Best, P. Wikipedia, retrieved October 08, 2009
http://en.wikipedia.org/wiki/Pete_Best#The_Pete_Best_Band

Phil Aspinall was one of the early producers of the Beatles and is thought to have been the father Roag, the younger brother of Pete Best. At the time of the first channeled message, I had no knowledge of the personal history of the Pete Best band. Roag was the son of Mona who owned the Casbah!

Photo: Marcia at George Harrison Days with "Beatle Bob Bartell"

This is a picture of Marcia with Bob Bartell, "Beatle Bob" from George Harrison days, 2008, in Benton, IL They are in front of the "Hard Day's Night Bed and Breakfast" where the Pete Best Band stayed and played for Harrison Days in Benton, Il, September 2008.

Bob Bartell is an author and a devoted Beatles fan, who saved the "Hard Day's Night Bed and Breakfast" from demolition in Benton IL. Bob comes from Springfield, IL.

John Lennon Speaks on Free Love, the Beatles and BBS Radio!

Channeled by Marcia McMahon, July 5, 2006

M: Dear John, well I'm here on the page and making

contact. How is life on the other side these days?

John: (Laughing) Pretty much the same dear Marcia.

George and I have been creating lots new music and will be

featuring it on your great show soon.

M. I got to thinking to ask Don to revise the music debut we

did so that it comes in loud and clear, as he said that some of

it was barely audible.

John: Yeah at the very least that should be done so that you

do get noticed as you are going to go big.

M: You keep telling me that John. I suppose Bob Murray

"will go big" since it's his music. I would like the lyrics out

there in the mass consciousness. There is now such a profound

need for peace. We have Israel and Palestine on the verge of

war, and the North Korean dictator launching missiles on the

105

fourth of July. Seems to me that there are nations around the world that want aggressive military action, besides the United States, which feels entitled to military action.

John: Your message and your work couldn't be more important than now, especially since Diana's words can prevent terror on America. I'm not a patriotic sort as you know, and was the rebel spirit of the Beatles; but nonetheless, I don't want any more terror upon America, because America is the only free country among just a few.

We had to go big in America because that was where the future light workers of ascension would be. We had them in England too, the whole generation. But without the freedom there in America, there wouldn't have been "FREE LOVE".

Although it was Yoko and I—our dream on our honeymoon for God's sake—and it caught on in America. That is why so much channeling and work with angels is happening in America. America is the leader for all spiritual waves, and frankly BBS radio is the leader for radio in America. It's what every station should be. There are dark forces that don't want this kind of light work and peace work being done. We

applaud Don and his brother Doug for their efforts. We'd like

to see all his shows out there but particularly yours Marcia,

since it can have a wide reaching effect of peace, both through

the music and through Diana's words being read on the air.

M: Well John that's quite a compliment. I 'm going to

share this with our producer Don Newsome and I think he'll

feel well pleased with his extraordinary efforts.

John: By all means share my thoughts with your friend

Don, with my blessing, and remember all you need is Love!

M: Thanks for your communication here John. I look

forward to more music with Bob Murray.

John: Yeah we'll be sending it through Bob. We'd like to

ask our listeners to please call the station and request songs

during your reading time too. We want to put it out there and

really make an impact.

Marcia: I'll mention it to Don. Thanks again John!

John: You're welcome. Remember peace! Remember Love!

Ciao and bye for now,

John

Notes: Bob Murray is the medium/channel that channels the music inspired by John Lennon and George Harrison, while I am channeling the lyrics to Bob's songs. Bob can be found at www.thestarsstillshine.com and you can select your favorite song from that site all for free! You do know that by now; but references still need to be given.

Don and Doug Newsome are the founders of BBS radio. Marcia McMahon, M.A, hosts the Peaceful Planet Radio show, The Peaceful Planet used to air Saturdays on BBS, www.bbsradio.com At 2:00 pm central time. Marcia's website: www.dianaspeakstotheworld.com is where you can also read John's other messages. There are also my channeled portraits in watercolor of John, all inspired by his spirit.

References: Murray, B. retrieved October, 09 www.thestarsstillshine.com

John Lennon on Ascension and Peace
Channeled March 14, 2007

Marcia: Hi John; I'm hearing ya John.

John: Yeah, Marcia my dear, long time no channeling babe!

We understand you're trying to get the show back up and finish the first chapter of your book with me. It's a huge project, but you will get there as you were meant to channel me years ago. When spirit wants something done, they chose a busy person.

M: John was that you coming thru with the song I heard today, Revolution?

John: Just a way to wake you up a bit to make you realize that everything right now is undergoing some serious change. The earth as she prepares for Ascension is intending to pull light workers and peace workers together for the common cause of peace.

I am, for one, delighted to see you working with the family you had on your show who have so much good intention and good will for humanity. I am aware of their projects and have been involved with them for a while now, though I know we're not saying much until the second book.

It's not like me to hold back, but I would like to suggest you both collaborate and include Bob Murray. They have contacts you'll need and you have contacts they'll need to get this project off the ground, so to speak.

M: Are you seeing a possibility of a publisher, John, for the book?

John: In time yeah, when you are out on TV there will be many stepping forward to help your cause for peace. We cannot say for sure that the one you are submitting to now is the right one, but it's a good bet. We certainly hope so, as we wanted this project for Peace out Yesterday!

Well please do set aside time whenever you can, Marcia my dear, to do the music lyrics as there is far more to it than you ever thought. We're so glad to be working with you and don't

110

give up on the world and on peace; it couldn't be more

important now.

By the way, say hello to Barry Eaton, [Eaton, B.

www.Radiooutthere.com] *he, too, is a wonderful light worker*

and producer and he is an enlightened soul who wants, in

some way, to help the project.

Ciao for now.

Luv ya,

John

Notes: In 2007 I appeared on Barry Eaton's' Radio Out
There online from Australia. I've been a featured guest of
Barry's for more than 4 years now. Barry is a wonderful
interviewer and has a strong vocal presence, is very sharp and
his years of experience at ABC news stand out for having
served the mainstream media in Australia. He is a great
interviewer and host.

References: Eaton, B. www.radiooutthere.com

The Beatles and Ascension

Notes: I find it really interesting that John says the Beatles were paving the way for Ascension in the last sample channeling from John. What is Ascension? If you aren't New Age you have no doubt heard of the Ancient Mayan Calendar as it relates to the prophecy of 2012. It is a timeline with a lot of prophecy attached to it that is very popular right now, as we approach the 2012 timeline. Is it the end of the world? I have my own thoughts on this; and so does John. Though the calendar was written in stone thousands of years ago it does predict an end game to earth, and a solar alignment with a Hunab Ku; a Mayan equivalent of our own Galactic Center; said to align perfectly on Dec 21, 2012. This was not well understood—that there even was a Galactic center which is a giant rotating black hole—until fairly recently. The Mayans were mathematical geniuses and they were prophecy keepers as well.

The Hunab Ku is said to be the center of the galaxy and also of divine energy. As the Maya understood it, when earth aligned to that Galactic center it would usher in the so-called 5th world. We speak today of the 5th dimension; and I understand that to be a place of the angelic realms. John is speaking to me from the 5th dimension, as I understand it. This Galactic energy, spoken of in my work with Archangel

Michael, will align with the earth as she passes through Full
Aquarius on Dec 21, 2012.

Ascension is a movement in the New Age that prophesies
everything from the end of the age, to the beginning of the
Golden Age, everything from doom and gloom to Golden Age
is centered on the date 2012. Great earth changes, solar wind
and flares and Galactic Energy from our Source coming to
earth at the time will bring change of unprecedented nature;
and events in our world point to that happening. Look at the
number of earthquakes, today's date being March 3, 2010.
Archangel Michael has spoken through me and other channels
confirming there will be more earth cleansings.

Many psychic channels have predicted everything from
massive earth changes, tidal waves, and tsunami to total
collapse of the Earth. Others claim that while the earth lines
up in Aquarius astrologically speaking; there will be deadly
cosmic rays from our own center of the galaxy which will
penetrate the earth leaving nothing here. What to make of all
of this? I believe those of us who want to, will have an
opportunity to move up in vibration with the ascension
movement will to the 5th dimension. There are preparations
needed to ascend; it is not a gift to be taken lightly.

I do know and understand it to be the opening of the 4th and
into the 5th dimension. As to the vast earth changes, who can
deny that tsunamis, tidal waves, volcanoes, earthquakes and

other perplexing earth changes are all happening? Could this be culminating in an end time scenario around the 2012 timeline? (Evers, C. retrieved Dec 9, '09) "I believe something is up with planet earth, don't you?" (McMahon, M. lyrics, 2012)

These scenarios will have to unfold as they are destined to do. John seems very excited about Ascension. Every time I have asked him, he seems to feel that it is a Golden Age about to be born, and references Ascension in his messages and even his lyrics. Formally speaking, the term ascension means, quite simply to move up in life forms from one dimension to the next. The energies from our own sun will so powerfully ignite our souls that the whole solar system will possibly shift to the 5th dimension, allowing humankind the opportunity to shift with the earth into the 5th dimensional awareness.

This will ignite our vibrations beyond anything imagined thus far except for those few avatars who walked the planet and ascended before us, such as Jesus the Christ, and Sai Baba, Baba gi, Mother Mary, Buddha and other well-known Ascended Masters. As they ascended they took their bodies with them. Some thinkers and authors I've interviewed believe this will be possible at that vortex in time.

There is more to it, and John has not left this difficult subject for us to ponder alone. One such example is called Radical Dolphin. (See the musical lyrics at the end of this book.)

References: Evers, C. The 2012 Countdown website, www. The2012Countdown.com retrieved Dec 9, '09 thoughts and ideas are referenced from Carolyn's work

McMahon, M. www.dianaspeakstotheworld.com my messages from RA, The Heavenly Host, and Archangel Michael, all of whom I also work with.

McMahon, M. **Ascension Teachings with Archangel Michael**, 2012. My new e book released in 2012 describes this fascinating and mystical process in detail. Online at www.angelfire.com/mb2/diana_speaks/archangelmichaelsmes sages.htmland and at amazon.com.

John Speaks on the Hugh Reilly Liquid Lunch Show

Channeled Sept, 2009

Marcia: Dear John, it's been so long since we've spoken and now a wonderful opportunity arises with an invitation from the great Hugh Reilly to appear on www.thatchannel.com and bring thru your music and message John. I apologize I've been too busy to connect to your love and music lately. But I am excited for the 9-9-9 release of the Beatles new CD.

Anyway John, how are you there?

John: OK luv, coming on thru John hear. Sometimes it's hard to hear you your vibration is so soft and gentle. Yeah, I wan to be on Hugh's show; he's fantastic! And to think it's gonna be live, like TV. This is a great opportunity, ya know, to bring people to the awareness of the great music you and Murray are doing for the world. Even though you're not currently on the air, Marcia, I did predict you'd go big. And

116

when I say big I don't mean like the Beatles big; I mean

among your own kind. Everyone will have heard now of our

music from the Half Beats and George too!

Not all will accept this I realize, but that is not my concern

nor should it be yours. Just let them enjoy the great tunes

we've been creating thru Bob Murray. I do predict a contract

of some sort will come out of this one, my dear. Bob's got to be

on the show, too. Maybe Hugh can have you on and then Bob

on in the same sequence--just a thought for continuity's sake.

We love you both and want your lyrics and Bob's music out

there!

We've been waiting such a long time, really, for folks to

know about this project. Unfortunately other moviemakers and

people who don't really channel me have tried to cash in on

the Lennon legend.

Marcia, my dear, you've never done this for money. That is

why a person of such integrity deserves to be known; not for

my name alone but for the creative effort and talent you do

channel.

Anyway, as you can see I'm a little excited about being on air again just like Ed Sullivan; who is creating his new show on this side called Dead on Ed Sullivan. George and I were on a few weeks ago to commemorate Diana. They had a children's celebration and we provided some of the music; so did Elvis.

Bob can share all that with you, luv.

Well, luv, we're in studio today and working on more songs to send to Bob. Pease do tune in more often. I wondered what had become of you, luv.

Don't give up hope that someday, luv, the songs will all be known and sung in peace and love

Luv

John and George

Notes: Bob is of course Bob Murray, on
www.thestarsstillshine.com who channels the music of John
Lennon. Bob always writes about what George and John are
doing on the other side and includes their adventures on the
other side in his ezine; called the Stars Still Shine Ezine. It's a
funny and heartening read. Bob had to ok the project of my
appearance before I could share the music of John on air. I
believe we aired on Sept 23rd, 2009 on the Hugh Reilly show
on www.Thatchannel.com which is a filmed radio tv outlet in
Toronto, CA. Hugh does a great job and was thrilled to have
John's spirit on and available for comment although there
were questions John did not want to answer. Hugh was
gracious enough to allow John to speak on his own, so to
speak, through me!

News and Writings from the Afterlife by Robert Murray. A Message from John Lennon

T H E S T A R S S T I L L S H I N E M A G A Z I N E

www.TheStarsStillShine.com/zine.html

The Stars Still Shine Magazine, a monthly e-mail. Publication is a direct link from the afterlife. It is an outlet for talented writers and other "people" in spirit. They share messages, conversations, stories and journeys filled with descriptions of adventure and travel. These writers and others from the afterlife channel through Robert Murray. ISSN: 1543-0022

Editor's Notes: The following articles are new and are from the Other Side.

* An article from the December 2005 issue (Vol. 3 Issue 12) of "The Stars Still Shine Magazine." http://www.TheStarsStillShine.com/zine.html

2. SPECIAL—MESSAGE

A Message from John Lennon.

December 2, 2005

To Murray from John

I'm not religious in a conventional way. I believe in God.

How could you not when his wonders are all around us? I've experimented with different religions and different ways of living and now death. I am most upset when human beings decide to wage war on other human beings. In the old days, before my time, humans used to kill each other, invade other lands, enslave people and behave in a terrible way. Now we have antiseptic wars where the originators of the invasions sit back in relative comfort and have their armies do the terrible deeds. We now have become very good at getting out the publicity to justify the wars. Any form of offensive war is not and cannot be justified, period. For Heaven's sake and for Earth's sake, give peace a chance!

I've been sending Murray some songs that I put together. He ran into a snag with getting out the music and needs an agent. I don't see any problems from where I am but I do remember some very hot arguments about getting some of our songs out to the public. There always seemed to be some log thrown across to make us [The Beatles] take our time. Murray tells me that he is going to put the Lennon Music on his web site and make some kind of arrangement for people to listen to it without paying. I don't think that's going to work but I'm willing to do my part. Keep it in your heads that it takes more than money to promote world peace. Maybe the music could remind you to do something about peace. You know, even a short prayer would help.

I guess I'm getting mellow. (Although George seems to think that I've gone cranky lately. I'm willing to wait for Murray to get the music straightened out. Although I'm not one to explain my actions to anyone, I want people to understand where I'm coming from. I want you to feel my frustration! I'm not expecting peace to come over the world tomorrow but I do want to see a real start towards peace. I've had some heavy arguments with Lady Diana, and she is a lady. We do agree that there should be peace in the world but can't agree on the way to do it. She concentrates on children and I want to do it through music. We agreed that all legitimate means to get world peace have a place. She is so intense that I think she's going to burst into flames at any moment. I'm not, of course. I'm calm, cool and laid back—

NOT!

I heard a story about a man, a real cool man, who spent

some of his time in jail because he refused to pay his taxes.

(Henry David Thoreau) His country was warring against the

natives. He didn't want his money to go to war so he didn't pay

his taxes to the government. Maybe that's a dumb idea but at

least he felt he was doing something to promote peace. What if

everybody felt the same way he did? What if everybody

withheld the taxes that paid for a war? That was a question

not a suggestion. There are other ways you can help. Think!

Think then do something n a constructive way!

With LOVE, LOVE, LOVE, PEACE, PEACE, PEACE,

John

* An article from the January 2006 issue (Vol. 4 Issue 1) of "The Stars Still Shine Magazine." http://www.TheStarsStillShine.com/zine.html reprinted with Permission from Robert Murray.

John Lennon Speaks Out on War in the Name of God

Channeled by Marcia McMahon, Jan 14,2009

www.dianaspeakstotheworld.com

M: Hi John, well I'm here on the page finally for you and for the start of the book.

John: Yeah, Marcia, I'm right here and I've been waiting for your call for weeks now. We've got real work to do, my luv, and I'm ever pleased to see you turning on your high school students to my great Beatles tunes, as well as James Taylor. One small point to remember, luv, is that James is not your favorite singer dear it's really me, luv. Oh yeah

She loves you yeah, yeah, yeah.

Well you know what I mean; all those lyrics get stuck in your head and really help uplift your spirits in the dead of winter. I know cuz one of my main reasons for continuing on with you is the music and the book. It's not like I do not have other channels but you are special Marcia. You have risen above the crowd mentality and don't look for the mass

124

consciousness to approve you because you have your own

inner joy and confidence that what you do is genuine.

So I want to say to people to seek the truth on their own,

independent of the lies of religion and the lies of the society as

a whole.

The mass culture is so distorted creating all these wars and

lies in the name of God.

I hate the idea of God being used as a battering ram to the

people of the Middle East and using God as an excuse to kill

people. It's positively sick ya know.

So while Diana has had a lot to say about Gaza, lately,

both on your show and up here; we're all for you both, as both

of you are fine peace workers. And we want an end to all

military wars masquerading as just wars. It's terrorism to

bomb innocent people.

Well, I know I'm getting all upset just thinking about the

numbers coming over here daily--women and children, you

know. I do not want to offend any Jewish person with my

comments as I hold every religion in the same place--they are all a little off!

But by the same token we ask all people everywhere to insist on peace and love and to insist that your government stop the war and killing in the name of God.

I have touched the Divine coming from this side and the Divine would never think of war.

I hope you all do your part for peace before it's too late and do tune into the wonderful new tunes on the Peaceful Planet show.

Luv ya

John

Notes: This was channeled in during the horrific bombing of the people of Gaza by Israel last January. John was emphatic that he not offend any religious person in the message. I am not able to edit that out of the message due to the fact that is the way it was received. He does get political, as in life! Remember that John's political views are not always my political views.

John on the Indigo Crystal Children
Channeled November 2008

Dear John;

Marcia: Well here I am I know you've been around a for a good while and I appreciate you and your being a great guide. You must have wondered whatever happened.

John: Marcia, my dear, I am taking a break right now with George who says hello. We lads are both raring to go on your show once more with our newest tunes for peace; when you have a moment we'll be glad to channel them in. I really do understand your being overworked and know that you've got to make a living. And in the Mid-west, where you are, teaching art is the best job, if you have to have a job.

While it won't last forever since you deserve retirement from all that crap with the school, and on and on, the kids will, in time, luv ya. Be gentle with them as they are all special kids, as you know these days. They are here to help us in Ascension and came with a mission. And they don't relate well to rules and the usual crap that schools try to bring upon their

127

little heads. They need lots of freedom, lots of technology and lots of music with their art. Don't make them do art without talking. Find a happy medium. I know I am a bit of a free spirit and you have to run the classroom, and it frustrates you when they misbehave. But hell they're only kids once! And so be gentle and don't' let them put you in the corner of the room at your desk. Get up and be ONE with them, learn to laugh and don't' worry what the other teachers think; they're really not on your level there at all. Be gentle and Love is all you need. The new crystallines are so amazing. Just share in the glory of creating art.

George says hello and not to give up on the BBS network; Don will help you on your new project.

Ciao for now,

Luv you,

John

Note: Much has been said in other books about the Indigo children. If you just do a Google search you will find at least ten or more books out now about them. They seem to come in with God-given psychic ability and intolerance for rules. The Crystals are also amazing because they are the sons and daughters of Indigos and they are now growing up in junior high and high school. I found them interesting as young artists.

Natalie Glasson, www.natalieglasson.com seems to fit the category of an Indigo child who is bringing in the most exquisite messages on ascension. So many are awakened to spirit and enlightenment!

Happy New Year from John Lennon
Channeled by Marcia McMahon, Jan 5, 2008

Marcia: Hi John, sorry it's been so long channeling. It's not that I do not have an interest in what you are doing or saying John. I've been so busy.

John: Well we have been trying to reach you for a very long time. I did say thru Claudine that you are in fact working too hard and taking everything too seriously, as usual for you.

We do understand you have so many projects going and we commend them one and all. We ourselves had a great New Year's Eve party at the club and performed with Michael and the Band and for the many newcomers here that needed some cheering up.

We are still producing new songs thru Bob Murray and I am also glad to hear you are in touch with many of my other channels throughout that world.

Marcia: Can you say John about the music on the show and if we'll find a good producer and agent? We've been waiting, you and I, a long time now. Is the year 2008 the right time?

John: Your musical lyrics and Bob's music couldn't be more on time. As the Half Beats, George and I are determined to get our great sounds out to the world.

There was a situation last year we felt would develop for you. We do not know what may have happened, but we do see this work out there sooner than you think. In fact we see you, Marcia, out there on TV sooner than you think. With all your talent we'll so glad to see you are still on air with BBS radio.

We send out our special love vibration to all your listeners and to the great light worker, Don Newsome, who is doing so much to help Peace for the Planet. All we were saying is Give Peace a Chance.

And so we ask all you listeners to find ways to volunteer your efforts in any way you can, to assist the suffering peoples of the world, such as Africa and all those in war torn countries, to go ahead and give generously. This will increase the love vibration for the whole planet.

Well, Marcia my dear, we are always here ready to hear you whenever you are feeling like a little song. George and I send on our love to ya and say Happy New Year 2008, a year of great surprises for all of you out there.

With love from me to you,

John Lennon

Notes: Newsome, N.D. retrieved Jan 2008, www.bbsradio.com

Don Newsome is the founder along with Doug, and the radio producer at www.BBSradio.com who gave me my first radio show, and then also the Peaceful Planet show. He helped me a great deal with archiving the music by Bob Murray and by giving me time slots that were prime time from the very beginning. Don is a true gem of a guy and a wonderful light worker.

John's Message—The Magical Musical Tour

Channeled Oct 7, '2009 (Phrase coined by Robert Murray,www.thestarsstillshine.com)

Marcia: Dear John: I'm seeing you in your old look this evening. You are showing me you are dressed like Sergeant Pepper's Lonely-Hearts Club Band. You've got your suit on and your spectacles, with your long hair. What's the message John?

John: Marcia darling, right here for you now. I've got to get your attention somehow on this project; to let you know that I'm delighted you are finally taking time out of your busy life to do this for George and me. It means more than you could know. But I'm dressed this way to show you our Magical Mystery Tour, or as Murray would say, Magical Musical tour! I want you to ask Murray for more of the songs on the Magical Musical Tour and get busy with channeling a few more tunes. You'll be amazed.

That was music George and I have written in the last few years. Do you realize it's been quite a few years since you've done much with the lyrics? And that is what you'll be known

for, dear. So just a bit of jest with you this evening, luv, to

encourage you to do more with lyrics. Don't worry about Bob.

He's very shy but a great channel and understanding. He'll go

along with the project if you have a publisher or an agent

behind you. He knows, then, they assume the greater share of

the risk; and that's what both of you two greats need, a good

agent, as I've been saying. Do you realize the trash that poses

as spiritual messages in the mass consciousness, and how

truly talented you and Murray are?

Well you better know that, luv, because you are a great

channel no matter what may have happened with Pete Best's

band. Not everyone is going to buy it, luv; but I am still here

to say that it's myself John and George. We're not the famous

Beatles anymore but we are the Half Beats and we're very

determined to get peace for the planet. We'll do it, luv, just you

see.

All my luv,

John.

Notes: Bob Murray is the channel for the Magical Musical Tour and he coined the phrase.

Did you detect the old Beatles humor and use of wording? It's all John's creativity as it comes through. He has used the words he wants to portray this project through Bob Murray and myself. There is no attempt to use anything but the original words we receive from John in spirit.

References: Murray, R. retrieved Oct 9, 2009 www.thestarsstillshine.com all rights reserved.

http://www.TheStarsStillShine.com/musicbuy.html

John: http://www.thestarsstillshine.com/musicbuy.html#jl

George: http://www.thestarsstillshine.com/musicbuy.html

John's New Year's Message; Expect the Unexpected!

Channeled Jan 2, 2010

Marcia: Dear John; I am here on the page typing and editing; really hoping to get this manuscript ready for the agent. Happy New Year it must be that 2010 is destined to be yours John.

John: Darling, it's great to hear your vibration. I have to adjust my earphones as we're rehearsing for a special show we're gonna do for Diana and the children soon. George and I came up with it, of course with Lady Diana's urging.

M: Gee does that sound familiar John. So glad you mentioned Diana, I've been meaning to connect to her soon too.

John: She sends her love to you, Marcia Darling. She is a darling herself as she has so much love for the children. The show is all about what you can do for peace, and to help others even in a small way. Mother Teresa is assisting Diana in the project. Well anyway George and I got roped into it so to speak. We're really glad to be of help to the great Lady Diana anyway and it's always a pleasure to work with her. She is a bit driven, as you are, you know, luv.

I want to wish you the very best New Year and all your listeners and readers.

Things here are going on and of course George and I have more lyrics to channel in whenever you find a spare moment. I think you better learn to slow down and listen to your inner voice more this year and take time to do those things you love, for all the hard work really isn't worth it without friendships my dear.

Just a bit of advice here: You do enjoy people so get out of the house more and drop in on other events where you can. Don't spend all day and night on the computer as you have in past years. You have an extraordinary year ahead and I'm not gonna reveal all of it now; but to say to expect the unexpected!

You'll be all right if you do decide to change things a bit, and you'll be bored if you stay. But I understand how unstable the economy is right now, luv, so you've got to do what's best for survival too.

George says hello and would like to request a special session with him soon, for a message back home as he put it.

Marcia: John that's quite an honor. I'll be glad to offer my ear to George.

John: I thought so, luv. Well we're in the studio with more songs for the children so I'll say goodbye, luv, and wishing you the very best of luck with the book!

I think, my dear Marcia, you'll get there if you take an hour a day! No more than that, luv. Too boring. You have got to remember to get out of the house.

Remember peace. Remember love

With love,

John

Notes: In this message from John he was right on again. In 2010 I was diagnosed with late stage breast cancer. That must have been the "unexpected" he was referring to. I later had a recurrence to a brain tumor, and that is why I was not able to type or finish the book until now. I lost the use of my right hand to a brain tumor but I have recovered completely from cancer as of this writing.

A New Message from George about the Web site and Tape titled "The Beatles Never Broke Up"

Channeled Jan. 2010

George: George here. This is a great project you're on for world peace with John. I'm in the background cheering you both on. Naturally, I want it to succeed and can also help you with your work. I personally did not like the idea of the Best Band doing our work since it's so spiritual these days and focused on Ascension. John agrees it 's focused on Ascension but he feels, maybe, more inclined to like to relive the past Beatles history with the old sounds we did in the sixties and seventies. I am one for moving forward with time and with new styles.

M: If I may say so George your work is astounding and just takes me breathless! I could hear the love and the slightly eastern instruments as soon as I heard it was you. The love also comes through your work and it's better than anything you did, if you'll pardon my saying so, on the earth plane!

George: Flattery will get you everywhere! Laughing but really yeah I agree with you.

The stuff we are creating now is so focused and so spiritual and it's so great to have John by my side writing again. As for being all together in some other dimension well, as I was telling Bob Murray the other night; that guy James has a lot of nerve telling people he got picked up by UFO's and then stealing our riffs and mixing them with other stuff for a sound alike contest. Yeah; yeah yeah! That was a lot of rubbish and I'm glad Fr. Murray knows a dead fish when he can smell it!

Marcia: You got me going on that idea George. Though I do believe in other dimensions and aliens, the combo there was too darn much to believe!

George, I am not interested in doing any Beatles sound alike contest. What Murray and I are up to is actually being present to your vibrations so that we can be of service to you and John and be a scribe to the lyrics. I absolutely loved the lyrics to Something for Gossamer Wings and a few others of your tunes.

George: Thank you; thank you very much! Elvis has left the building and so must I, soon, do the same, Marcia. It was great to speak with you, dear lady. Good luck on the project and we'll be rooting you on from the upstairs studio.

Marcia: If you see Diana tell her I have not forgotten our work and will connect soon.

George: Will do; much love to you and peace!

Love, George.

Notes: I can't help but notice George's great sense of humor about the website posted by some anonymous guy claiming to have been contacted by aliens and lifted into another dimension where the "Beatles never broke up!" Maybe you thought doing lyrics with John and George was stretching it, but that to me is really stretching the limits of the imagination! I don't judge the unusual or paranormal knowing I work with it.

But after hearing the music it did appear to have riffs from old Beatles tunes and uncanny sounds similar to old Beatles music. George must have been a funny guy and strikes me less serious than John. But George is known for his amazing dedication to Hindu philosophy and enlightenment. I loved getting this message as it struck me for his humor and wit. I was delighted to hear from George after hearing his lyrics in my head for many years the honor was all mine that night.

References: The Story of the Tape: author unknown. N.D. Retrieved Jan 2010. The Beatles Never Broke Up Website: http://www.thebeatlesneverbrokeup.com/index.php? option=com_content&view=article&id=1&Itemid=53

John Lennon Speaks on the Anniversary Dec 8, 2009- Love is All You Need!

Channeled by Marcia Dec 8, 2009

Hello John. I know it's your anniversary and I wanted to check in with you and say how much we all loved you and still do John.

John: Marcia, my luv, you are great to stop in and say hello; I know you're busy on Christmas and all the responsibilities you do have daily. Don't forget you can set aside an hour a day and get the book to our mutual friend, Julian soon.

M: Knowing how your fans feel about the great loss of your talent and your physical presence here, is there something you want to convey to the fans John? There are many on my email lists that want to know what's up with you?

John: Yeah, we've said so much before; that I will always love my fans. After all being a Beatle and singing about love was what I came for. I was one of the luckiest persons in the world. Of course I never knew it as I had so many things going in my life. I loved them all- no pun intended but I loved song writing the most with Paul. I used to write the poems and Paul would work on the musical part; then I'd get on with that and back and forth. We spent many hours in the studio doing that. It took a while to write some of the better songs we are known for.

M: Yes, and what about now John? I know you are writing more tunes through several of your channels. I love everything you've sent me but Radical Dolphin happens to be a favorite. It has a flavor of Yellow Submarine a bit, with the references to the sea and waves.

John: Well George and I are writing songs all the time now and we've done much more since you've taken time to channel the lyrics. Bob has channeled some lyrics into the songs, as you know. When time permits we'll send more lyrics to ya.

M: John are there any other messages for today?

John: At this point I really want people to understand the importance of world peace and that with Ascension around the corner; we've got to get there. We can't allow for any more justifications for war; including the war in Afghanistan. Terrorism is a complex issue I know and understand; that it must be met in different ways. Love is the answer to terrorism, just love everyone and don't destroy people because that isn't love. No God or Divine Creator would possibly want you to kill your brother or mother or whatever. It's got to be understood in that part of the world; and maybe that's a job for you and Diana. As for me truth has always been simple. Love is all you need.

On that note I wish to say to my fans that if they have love in their hearts that is all they need to progress, and do what they want to do. Please turn on to peace before it's too late.

All my loving,

John

P.S. George sends his love to all his fans too!

John and George of the Half Beats

References: Channeled on the anniversary date of the tragic loss of our beloved friend John. He had spoken before about the importance of love in his earlier messages, as well as his role as a Beatle. This message is directed to his fans, but also confirms his strident efforts for peace even from the afterlife.

PART TWO:

LYRICS TO THE MUSIC

Notes: Presented here are the lyrics to Bob Murray's songs as inspired by John or George. We can't claim John or George wrote these songs due to copyright law. But we ask you to consider our limited imagination as both of us are teachers by trade and don't write this well. Perhaps you can hear John or George in some of the lyrics and get your own sense of their presence with us as we composed these works.

A few of the songs have been created with the help of those gifted in music and are on the mp3 files of my program, the Peaceful Planet. John gave the idea of the Peaceful Planet as the title for my show, which we play at the start of the show each week.

It was the first song I channeled in from spirit in 2005, way before I ever had a radio show, and gives you an idea about John's intensity to put the word out with his intentions. However I take full credit for the lyrics, which are channeled as I listen to the music I am able to connect to John's and George 's vibration enough to hear the words as they are intended to be harmonized and produced for the purpose solely of bringing people into world peace and Ascension. Robert Murray holds all copyrights on the music and if you have not yet checked out his musical creations on his site, please visit **www.thestarsstillshine.com** where you can hear sample songs for free. Neither Bob nor myself are a musician but we are attempting to honorably present the work of the

Half Beats, from spirit. I hope after you read through the lyrics you will "hear" John or George's presence style, and influence in the words. We make no claims other than these are the words as channeled from spirit! I am particularly fond of the songs Appreciated Angels, and Remarkable Nebulae, as well as Prelude to Savannah. Those songs are regularly played on the show.

HOW DO YOU ORDER THE MUSIC?

Visit Bob's site to listen to the musical creations for free or a small download fee. Alternatively, you can order a CD archive from the Peaceful Planet show, through me at marciadi2002@yahoo.com. The CD's are in the original unedited format in mp3 files and are an hour long to include fabulous interviews on other topics to include ascension, world peace, Princess Diana and other masters messages and topics. Visit my site to order artwork of John at www.dianaspeakstotheworld.com, visit the ascended masters pages to order an original print of some of my paintings inspired by John Lennon.

You can also visit www.bbsradio.com and order archived shows of the peaceful planet.

Buy the music and listen to samples. To listen, click on the link for each song and a new page will open.

http://www.TheStarsStillShine.com/musicbuy.html

John: http://www.thestarsstillshine.com/musicbuy.html

George: http://www.thestarsstillshine.com/musicbuy.html

References: Murray, R. copyright www.thestarsstillshine.com music. All rights reserved, Robert Murray.

The Peaceful Planet
© By Marcia McMahon All Rights Reserved!

Lyrics Transcribed by Marcia McMahon© 2005

We live in peace in peace as One,

Over all the earth Ya Know,

To be as One to live as One,

Wherever we may go.

We live in peace forever more,

No more fighting no more wars,

No more attack, no more bloodshed

We celebrate the One God!

God is love, we've all been told

Each in our different ways,

We proclaim love and an end to war

Forevermore at peace.

The Peaceful Planet is being born being

Born from within us.

Begin to see, begin to feel

That all is One Around Us!

We proclaim that Love is One,

That we are all One in Divine Love,

We proclaim love

Forevermore the Peaceful planet.

We sing as One

Please sing along, we are the Peaceful Planet!

Right from within

Each in our way,

We proclaim the Peaceful Planet!

We know that we are One

No more use for toys of war;

No suicide bombs,

And no more terror!

For all religions simply ban it!

153

We proclaim that we are One; One in truth and love

Live in love and peace today, and

You'll have done your part

In creating the Peaceful Planet.

From John May 23, 2005

Radical Dolphin

(Influence- John) channeled by Marcia June 2005

Music © by Bob Murray, <u>www.thestarstillshine.com</u>

Radical Dolphin, swimming the seas

Knows something's up with earth,

Sees and feels it's true.

Swimming along in the deep blue

Shimmering waters,

Covering the earth,

Seeing something feeling something is

New, about to be born.

Swimming along feeling it's true,

Singing its song; making harmony of the seas

Gliding thru oceans and reefs,

The Radical Dolphin knows something's up,

Something's coming to earth.

Swimming the seas, knowing the breeze

Knowing the tides, the peaceful blue

Waters tell us something's different here.

A whole new way, a whole new day,

Sunshine and sea, waves and vibrations of the deep

Radical dolphin carries the codes deep within the seas,

Churning underground underwater,

Knowing its true, knowing it's blue

The New Earth is being born!

Radical dolphin speaks to man,

When will the wars end, the poisons of the seas?

When will it end? What price to pay for ocean's clean?

The radical Dolphin swims in pollution and waste,

When will the human race awaken to Ascension?

When will it be safe for habitation for man?

And beast?

The dolphins proclaim peace throughout the ocean's

waves,

And ask no more sonar waves from war machines

But ask for peace. All is One and all is well

Here in this little sea as she swims

In fun and laughter in the days,

Asking for peace, letting it be,

We ask for peace for

Radical Dolphin.

Let the sun shine down on

Dolphins, no more wars no more

Harm to oceans bright; let the New Earth be born!

Radical dolphin knows it's so,

So can you do your part to help the planet!

Save the whales and dolphins!

Radical Dolphin knows it's true,

Deep in the blue.

*Deep down inside, where we can hide from the tops of the
waves*

Fun in the deep, we keep promises to the dolphins

Radical dolphin knows it's true!

Down in the deep blue,

Something new being born.

Radical dolphins smiles up at you

Deep from the blue of oceans.

Notes: Let me quote my lyrics here to get the gist of ascension references, John said,

"Let the sunshine down on

Dolphins, no more wars no more

Harm to oceans bright; let the new earth be born!"

Notes: The New Earth is collectively known in ascension or New Age circles as a 5th dimensional earth that is possibly more etheric, and hence referenced as the New Earth.

There are even books entitled "Children of the New Earth" and I have channeled information about the New Earth. It's a big deal and no one in mainstream media will touch it. The End of the World as we know it brings shock and terror to the mortally minded. To the spiritually minded, it does not imply that; on a spiritual level it implies a New Earth one of love and justice. That is the hope anyway! John's lyrics confirm "Something's up with Earth, and New Earth is being Born." I leave that to reader discretion. I presented the lyrics here to analyze them in a deeper meaning that John may have in mind. We'll have to wait and see how the New Earth is born.

The many shifts in the earth's crust continue to be part of this Earth's ascension process and will be with us up until 2012, as his more recent predictions have indicated. He has recommended we learn to go within to hear Mother Earth. That is a subject perhaps for another book.

Reciprocated Sonnets
© By Marcia McMahon All Rights Reserved!

This sonnet's for you and you know it's true

It's reciprocated from me to you

We walk in love and peace

Along the beach singing our songs

Letting things go as they are

We walk along singing our songs.

Sonnets of true love

We have love within us

All that we ever need to know

Cuz all is within us—for all time now.

Believe that peace and love are in you.

You go along with that feeling all day

Making a song living in love and freedom,

The way that love is

From me to you with love it's true

Now and forever more from me to you.

We are as One song now singing along from me to you

Sonnets of truth and love are forevermore true.

No time no place here just me and you on the beach.

We sing along, wading in water singing along.

Reciprocated Glances
© By Marcia McMahon All Rights Reserved!

This song is for ya, you know that it's true;

Believe in love and the truth within;

Believe that love and Oneness true;

You go along in the truth of Oneness,

Knowing that all will be One in time then

Reciprocated from me to you,

That's how this game is played,

Until all mankind realizes

That all are One on this side, One on your side,

Forever playing out my glances are for you,

And yours for me;

This game of love never ends

Reciprocated glances again and again!

We walk along the beach of life romantic lovers;

Forever in love with ourselves;

Reciprocated from me to you ya know

Reciprocated within one glance

Within one instant we know that we are One

That all light and love are now here.

Sing as One, please sing along with us

Reciprocated Glances for lovers

We are One in love and One forever more.

Being in love being in the thick of it

We walk along the beach

It's life in all forms and formats, Ones across the ages of

Sands of time,

Forever more for ya.

With love from John.

Remarkable Nebulae
© By Marcia McMahon All Rights Reserved!

Remarkable in every way perfect

The nebulae are shining bright beyond the sun.

Beyond the sun and stars are nebulae shining deep within

The center of the cosmos they are shining away,

Creating life and lives within a universe of time

Far away from us,

Yet close enough to see that there is more;

So much more than we could ever dream possible.

Imagine that we see something

A half a billion years ago

 Shining in the star clusters at night,

Remembering half a million light years away a speck of

Stardust shining out and singing for me, for you.

A way of looking up and seeing the stars shining away

In time, distant time and places within our system and beyond

it;

Remarkable in every way perfect, that is

How they shine forevermore.

Remarkable Diana
© By Marcia McMahon All Rights Reserved!

Remarkable in every way perfect Diana

Shining light behind the peaceful planet

She shines and shines, deep within;

A princess so real and bright,

A special person after my heart,

A princess real and true.

True, and real was she living in love and peace,

Giving all her stuff to her causes and the children,

She gave her rose of life.

Rose of life was she, a Princess whom I had not met till here,

But adored while watching her on earth.

An earth angel for the children,

Diana, sing a song of praise for her;

Beauty immortal she is all that could be.

In an England

What a miracle was she.

Now this great light is in heaven here along with me.

Lamented Affairs

Lamented affairs, oh wishing we had come further along

with our development

We are as One and knew life as it wasn't,

So I do regret those affairs I had, singing along in my old

way.

There is no way to become something other than I'd been.

Lamented affairs within my mind now

Knowing you had better things to do

Than run around chasing after something else.

Always the lure to beauty and to good looks, what can I say

now?

Nothing else can hurt you now that I'm gone,

I hope we stay friends forevermore my dear

But please forgive me, my wandering eyes and heart;

For I didn't mean it, not one bit.

My heart's forever yours

From me to you now,

For more as One within the heart here.

We are as One within love you know it;

Lamented affairs.

Silent Creatures

(Influence: Lennon)

Silent creatures sing along and laugh;

We sing along with the sea life singing quite a bit;

We sing along with life;

We walk along the beach

Singing songs of peace.

We sing aloud sometimes;

We sound alike in our different ways.

Silent creatures now sing,

Silent no more as they find a voice for themselves;

Please say it with me;

Silent creatures sing songs sing along with me!

I am John singing this one's for you, you and me

Cuz we are already One.

The creatures of the sea need help;

They ask nothing but the end of pollution and war.

Along with the planet,

We celebrate the life!

Song of Honey Rose (Influence: John)
© By Marcia McMahon All Rights Reserved!

This is a song of Honey Rose then

A song of love and light forever taking

Time away and love lost.

We were as One and now gone forever.

Dearest Yoko, Honey Rose!

You are my sweet one rose of my heart.

If you could be near me,

We are One in time,

One in love with Honey Rose, Honey Rose.

We are already in love, forevermore as One

Be peace for the planet in my name, John.

Yoko dear, Honey Rose, be peace as I place

This rose in your heart from me.

To ya loving Yoko, I sing forever

A song of Honey Rose, for you;

With love from John.

We're as One and lost forever Honey Rose,

Honey rose forever longing for ya still.

Now gone, my honey Rose, just accept this

It's from me Honey Rose forever me.

This is John my heart is within your heart

In this Honey Rose, Dear Yoko, I'm one,

One with you in love forevermore.

We celebrate the One Love

Of our dreams and hopes for peace on earth.

Still there's a chance for Honey Rose.

My love is ever with ya, Honey Rose;

My love forever with ya, dearest Honey Rose.

We are One until the end.

Love

John

Continued Flirtations
(Influence: John)

© By Marcia McMahon All Rights Reserved!

Continued Flirtations we

Sing along we are as One

We sing along we are as One.

Therefore we sing as One in chorus;

We sing along we share a song

A glance, a flirtation here and there;

Forever we continue our flirtations and our glances;

We know we are falling in love.

Marcia McMahon

In love again

Forever in this place.

Heart and mind

Looking anew for love and an old one.

Forever we look on

Thinking we've lost and loved and lived;

And then it comes its way again.

Love all around ya, singing its own song;

We sing around the song of love that

Fills us and forms us and depletes us;

Until we find the continued flirtations again and again.

We sing and sing this song;

Continued flirtations around again.

Much love to ya,

John

Suspended Adventures
© By Marcia McMahon All Rights Reserved
(Influence: John)

Life had a suspended adventure for me;

I guess I never really thought that it could happen to me,

But it comes our way in time; all of us will find it.

Suspended Adventures, continue onward then

From here the place of heaven.

So many sages and wisdoms given to them over there;

But here I must say that I never expected to land here.

A suspended adventure; singing along a lonely song then

All by myself;

Singing along all by my lonely self.

Waiting, wanting to be free again,

Myself again, waiting for you to come

But then I find that self-pity can't bring me round at all.

I've got to go on and create, so then

Suspended adventure

Coming round again.

176

A way out and way in is through love within.

Don't' look to anyone or anything to give you that.

We all meet up with fate in one way or another again

So just rest assured we do all we can to help those are

On this side.

But we have limited capacity

In our adventures,

Not in imagination but in form.

In my form I could do whatever I wanted and I became

A legend in my own mind;

But then the adventures ended, leaving me in sadness and

confusion.

Don't waste time thinking what might have been,

For it's all in your head anyway.

Let peace and love in and forget the rest.

You'll know someday.

What I mean is live in peace and love and forget the rest.

177

Prelude to Savanna

(Influence: George)
© Music by Bob Murray, © Lyrics by Marcia McMahon
Let all rejoice in this good news:

All is Oneness, all is love, all is God.

Prelude to Savannah:

A prelude to Ascension on Earth.

Let us rejoice then as this is so:

A prelude to life unparalleled;

In Oneness no more wars, nothing but God's love for children

of the light everywhere.

Let it be said and said again, all is Oneness on this green

earth,

Prelude to Savannah, we all are One,

One is all.

Nothing stops the movement of peace and love

Now dawning upon this precious earth.

Let all rejoice that this is new,

A new beginning for earth is born.

Starting right within the heart of mankind, all we do is love.

Let all God's children rejoice now, the time of ascension is at

hand.

We can begin again a prelude to Savannah,

A prelude to peace.

Let all rejoice that this is God's plan,

For all mankind is born again,

Not in religion but in the heart of love for one another.

The hungry child in Africa, the aids babies,

All are brothers

Sisters all, let no one want for things of earth.

   Let all rejoice in love;

   Let the children sing along,

   Prelude to Savannah.

Passing Through Warm Places

(Influence: George)

Love is true, forevermore at peace ya know, I am eternal

In the love and light we know is true, passing thru the warm

places of my heart.

We rejoice in only love here; knowing this is true we are

eternal

Only love is true.

We rejoice in owning truth to heart here, only love is true.

You can look down on earth and see the children there, the

hunger there;

And see the smiles there when you can do something to help

assist the cause of peace. Only peace is true.

We are traveling thru warm places, only love is true

We can see that only love is true, passing thru warm places,

only the heart is true.

We ask you to do today, what your heart says to do and ignore

the mind;

For each time you do something, let your heart sing out.

Passing thru warm places, only love is real.

Images of My Love
© By Marcia McMahon All Rights Reserved!

(Influence Harrison) © Music by Robert Murray, ©

Lyrics by Marcia McMahon

Images of love I gave her forevermore;

Forevermore from here in heaven is my home.

Images of love to her from my Patty dear

Given in a love embrace of sorts, I have dreamt of you and

Images of my love run through my mind from here.

Thinking of you dear

Images of love from me, George, to you.

Images of love forevermore so true

My heart sings with thoughts of love for you.

As I sing along, John is hearing too.

We sing for the club here my dear, and play with thoughts of

you forevermore;

From heaven here my dear dear Patty.

182

Can you hear me dear? I sing each night for you while you

sleep.

From within your mind hear me darling and know my heart is

true,

From forevermore my dear, in heaven

Where we can be as One in truth.

Appreciated Angels
© **By Marcia McMahon All Rights Reserved!**

(Influence: John)

Appreciate the angels in your life

Appreciate what we have done and are all about you now,

More than you can know the angels hover round you,

Helping more than you can appreciate.

Appreciate the angels more than you can ever know;

We appreciate the angels more.

There is a way to know the truth, truth is within.

Angels hover near all about us;

We know we are One in light and love.

We are One forevermore.

Appreciate the angels in your life, for you know that we don't

live forever.

Sometimes looking back I see the angels were there for me

In my life as John;

Marcia McMahon

For it's true that I can be an angel for you now, looking down

from this

State of glory as it were, looking down upon earth;

Lifting her up to a new place.

Wings of the angels bring peace again to earth

And we will know we are all as One.

Angels bring us peace; I'll be looking down from this

Exalted state, Appreciated Angels in my life

And now I see you all, looking down on you.

I'm an angel now, with love from John Lennon.

Something for Gossamer Wings

Sunlight glistens down upon a garden, still and beautiful in

morning's dew.

The Gossamer wings are there, glistening in sunlight,

Beautiful and happiness, the butterflies fly around happiness,

Sings of heaven's beauty and truth.

Bring us to peace today, on Gossamer wings—the wings of

angels.

Surround us all in light and love;

Bring us to peace on earth; gossamer wings envelop us in love

and light,

Shedding light upon our earth.

Bring us to the light of God; we are in the light of him.

Bring us to light on earth, no more killing no more war.

Gossamer wings envelop our earth, bringing all to quiet

beauty on our earth.

The Angels surround us all in wings of joy, spreading wings

over all

The people everywhere, gossamer wings of joy.

Let there be peace on earth, good will toward men.

No terror upon our precious planet;

Just live life in peace and love,

Knowing you're doing your part for humanity.

Let peace begin with me; let all humanity forget the pain.

As new energies, brought by the Gossamer wings of angels,

Down to earth, where we really need it;

Something for Gossamer wings.

Sunlight glistens down upon a garden still, beautiful in

morning's dew;

The Gossamer wings are there, glistening in sunlight dear for

All mankind is love, singing songs of heaven's beauty and

truth.

Something for Gossamer wings.

References:

Pete Best Band History, retrieved Feb 6, 2010

Wikipedia, http://en.wikipedia.org/wiki/Pete_Best

Feb 6, 2010. www.wikpedia.com has a section on the Pete Best band and I checked it after I channeled my message from John about the band. I had no clue about the one who Roag Best was. Roag is the son of Pete Aspinall, a manager for the early Beatles.

Evers, C. www.The2012Countdown.com retrieved Dec 9.09. Thoughts and ideas are referenced from Carolyn's work.

Harper, J., www.johnjayharper.com, Trance formers: Shamans of the 21st Century.

Reality Entertainment TV. www.realityentertainment.tv

Eaton, B. www.radiooutthere.com retrieved 2007. Barry Eaton produces Radio Out There online from Australia. I've been a featured guest of Barry's for more than four years now.

Glasson , N., www.natalieglasson.com, Natalie Glasson seems to fit the category of an Indigo child who is bringing in the most exquisite messages on ascension. So many are awakened to spirit and enlightenment!

McMahon, M.A. 2003, Princess Diana's Message of Peace, excerpt from p.72, Diana: Further Warning, Dodi: Message to Muslims, p. 69. McMahon, M. www.dianaspeakstotheworld.com: my Ascension messages from RA, The Heavenly Host, and Archangel Michael, with all of whom I work with in channeling. **With Love from Diana, Queen of Hearts, Messages from Heaven for a New Age of Peace.** Published 2005. Page 61, John Lennon on Creativity and Diana's Message (With Love from Diana). C.

McMahon, all rights reserved.
www.dianaspeakstotheworld.com, c. 2005. **Ascension Teachings with Archangel Michael**, by Marcia McMahon, c. 2012, available amazon.com or

www.angelfire.com/mb2/diana_speaks/archangelmichaels messages.html

Murray, R. http://www.thestarsstillshine.com Home of the Stars still shine, an Afterlife Journey by Robert Murray, and the music of the Dead on Ed Sullivan, and the Magical Musical Tour. *The Stars Still Shine* Ezine by Robert Murray. All rights reserved, c. 2008 Murray, B. retrieved October 09 www.thestarsstillshine.com. Buy music and listen to samples. To listen, click on the link for each song and a new page will open.

http://www.TheStarsStillShine.com/musicbuy.html

John: http://www.thestarsstillshine.com/musicbuy.html

George: http://www.thestarsstillshine.com/musicbuy.html

Newsome, D. and D. are the founders of BBS radio. Marcia McMahon, M.A, hosts *The Peaceful Planet* radio show; I am also the author of **With Love from Diana,** *Queen of Hearts*. *The Peaceful Planet* used to air Saturdays on BBS, www.bbsradio.com

The *Peaceful Planet* show offered a variety of New Age topics from music to ascension, as well as Princess Diana's words on world peace. Our goal is to return the world to peace as envisioned by the Divine plan. One radio show is not enough to do that; however, the intentions of peace in such a war-torn world cannot be relegated to a trivial pursuit.

White, S. photograph from Strawberry fields Taken August 11,2001 www.myspace.com/sunflowersherry

ABOUT THE AUTHOR

Marcia McMahon M.A., CCH, and Reiki Master

BA, Ursuline College; MA, Case Western Reserve University and The Cleveland Institute of Art. Diana Gallery Online; Show Host, the Peaceful Planet Show BBS radio until late 2008. Contact the author/artist for beautiful artwork and reviews **www.dianaspeakstotheworld.com**

Marcia teaches art Appreciation Humanities at an Online University since 2007. Marcia is an internationally recognized author, artist and radio show host and has her art in numerous private collections throughout the US, Europe, and Canada.

She was named in **Who's Who in the World for 2007** for her art teaching and her watercolors of Princess Diana. Her psychic work with Princess Diana is having an impact on world affairs in the Middle East through Diana's messages. Visit BBS radio and tune in to hear Marcia's show, www.bbsradio.com The Peaceful Planet, dedicated to bringing world peace.

In 2010, Marcia was diagnosed with stage- three-breast cancer, and then the cancer traveled to her brain, making it stage four. Her guides, including Archangel Michael and Princess Diana, guided Marcia to the correct medical healing. Marcia is perfectly well today. She specializes in helping other cancer patients with reiki.

Marcia continues to reach audiences on both radio and TV with her message and work for the world on behalf of world peace. Marcia's interviews have been described as "riveting".

Marcia has numerous appearances on international radio programs such as **Radio Out There and on Liquid Lunch with Hugh Reilly on TV.** Barry Eaton, of radio out there, said about Marcia's work, a riveting read and always a fascinating show and interview. More recently Marcia appeared as a guest on talkstorytv.com with Dorothy Mercer author and host. Reach Marcia at marciadi2002@yahoo.com.

17653735R00109

Made in the USA
Charleston, SC
22 February 2013